Śrī Lalitā Sahasranāma

With Text,
Transliteration and Translation
Edited by
SWAMI TAPASYANANDA

Sri Ramakrishna Math
MYLAPORE MADRAS 600 004

Published by
Adhyaksha
Sri Ramakrishna Math
#31, Ramakrishna Mutt Road
Mylapore, Chennai-600004
09498304690
publication@chennaimath.org
Online store: *istore.chennaimath.org*
Ebooks: *www.vedantaebooks.org*

First Edition, November 1988
Third Edition, Third Print, January 2024
4000 copies

ISBN: 978-81-7823-099-3

Printed in India at
Sri Ramakrishna Math Printing Press
Mylapore, Chennai-4

Contents

EDITOR'S PREFACE

The Introduction to this edition of Lalitāsahasranāma is taken from the now out - of - print translation of it by Prof.D.S. Sarma. In place of writing a new Introduction, we have adopted this, because it is a composition that cannot be excelled. It is an excellent, appreciative, but also critical, study of the Sahasranāma as a piece of Stotra literature and as an exposition of the philosophy of the Mother cult. It is both a historical and a doctrinal study of this worship of the Supreme Being as the Mother, which is current all over India in different forms. In the translation of the Nāmāvali (list of Nāmās) also we are very much indebted to Prof.Sarma, as many of the wordings of it are also taken from his translation. He has given only a very cryptic translation of each Nāma. We have expanded it to full salutation - form with the Text in Devanagari and Romanised script with diacritical marks and English translation. In the Text of the hymn in Devanagari script, we have put hyphens dividing long word - combinations. This is done only for the convenience of readers who are not familiar with Sanskrit. They have no grammatical significance.

Lalitā, the shortened form of Lalitā-ambikā, means the Playful One. Her play consists in creation, sustentation and dissolution of the universe as also the lifting of devotees from Saṁsāra (the cycle of births and deaths). She is therefore the Universal Spiritual Energy, one with the Supreme Being, and can therefore be contemplated upon and worshipped in Herself, even taken out of the intricate web of Paurāṇika narratives. An abstract doctrine, however, is not easily comprehensible to man ordinarily. It does not stir his mind. If he is to understand that this abstract doctrine denotes a Being who is conscious and worshipful, that Being has to be presented in human terms which anthropomorphises it but yet stimulates a sense of its Divine nature—its omnisicence, omnipotence, benevolence, adorable nature etc. This is what the Puranas and Tantras have done through their wonderful narrative, which some intellectuals, who cannot understand their psychological effect on their believers, stigmatise as cock and bull stories. From a purely historical point of view this may be so. But they forget that they are not meant to teach history, but to create an experience of an adorable Being and man's intimate relationship with that Being. This the Puranas and Tantras achieve through their narratives. Lalitāmbikā is one of the finest products of this line of thinking. She is depicted as the quintessence of spiritual sublimity and power, and having an enchanting form with special parphernalia, manifestations and achievements by way of destruction of the forces of evil and enhancement of the forces of good.

A word here about the philosophy of worship of the Divine as the Great Mother. To those brought up in Semitic religions, such a conception is wholly unacceptable. God can only be Father according to Christianity and the Great Creator according to Islam. They forget that all conceptions of the Deity in the human mind are anthropomorphic, and it is far more reasonable to conceive Him as Father - Mother than merely as Father. This is what the cult of Sakti has done. Śiva is Pure Being and Śakti is Pure Will Each is a complement of the other and if separated completely from the other, both will be mere fictions. Together they are the Cosmic Whole and what transcends it. Though intellectually analysable, they are factually one. Śri - Cakra is a diagramatic representation of the Alogical Śiva - Śakti, and Its cosmic manifestation, and Lalitāmbikā, the central dot in the diagram is a more concrete form of It as divine Personality for adoration, praise and meditation. This Sahasranāma is an important litany in the scheme of worship of the Supreme Power as Mother Lalitāmbikā.

The two Sahasranāmās popular among devotees are the Viṣṇu - Sahasranāma and Lalitā - Sahasranāma.

The first one occurs in the Anuśāsanika Parva of the Mahabhārata and the second in Brahmāṇda Purāṇa. Viṣṇu - Sahasra - nāma is the earliest of this kind of hymnology. Its style is epic and therefore simple, as it existed before the development of the ornate style of the Kavyas, which is reflected in Lalitā - Sahasranāma. This can be found from the number of syllable combinations in its words. In the Viṣṇu - Sahasranāma the largest number of words are three syllabled. Their number is 338. Following it come 273 words of four syllables, 228 of two syllables, 106 of five syllables, 34 of six syllables, 18 of eight syllables, and 3 of single syllable. In contrast to this, the Lalitā - Sahasranāma has got 72 sixteen syllabled, 242 eight - syllabled and 278 four - syllabled word combinations followed by 138 of three syllables, 122 of five syllables, 34 of six syllables, 7 of nine syllables, 3 of eleven syllables, 3 of twelve syllables, 2 of seven syllables, and 3 of a single syllable. The length of the word combinations and the abundance of various forms of Samāsa (compound words) and Alaṅkāra (figures of speech) are the characteristic of Lalitā - Sahasranāma whereas the Viṣṇu - Sahasranāma is noted for its verbal austerity and lack of embellishments. Extensive alliteration in the beginning of words is a common feature of all Sahasranāmās.

Viṣṇu-Sahasranāma does not attribute any particular abode to Viṣṇu. He is the Indwelling Spirit in all beings, and the whole cosmos constitutes His body. But the Lalitā - Sahasranāma gives several abodes to the Mother like Cintāmaṇigṛha, Jālandhara, Kadamba-vana, Malayācala, Mahākailāsa, Vindhyācala, group of fifty Pīthas etc. The description of the form of the Deity is very much anthropomorphic giving as it does detailed descriptions of the various parts of the body. In Viṣṇu - Sahasranāma bodily description is marginal only, just to show that besides being the all-pervading spirit, Viṣṇu is a Personality too , but there is nothing in it to equal the description of the enthralling beauty of Lalitāmbikā. In the Lalitā various exploits of the Devi like the destruction of Bhaṇḍa are given in the beginning itself. The Viṣṇu, though it refers to the Avataras, never gives any description of their exploits. It is concerned more with the attributes of the Divine. Unlike the Viṣṇu, the Lalitā gives elaborate references to ritualistic worship like Śrī-Cakra Pūjā, the paths of Samaya and Kaula and other details of the Mother cult. The chanting of this Sahasranāma is made the concluding part of the Śri-Vidyā Upāsanā, which includes also the repetition of Pañcadaśākṣarī mantra and Śrī-Cakrapūjā. But for those who have no competency and facility to observe all the three, chanting the Lalitā - Sahasranāma alone is considered sufficient.

It is declared by Hayagrīva, while imparting this litany to Agastya, that the recital of it with faith and devotion, accompanied with offerings of fragrant flowers on the Śrī-Cakra, is the best means for man to attain all the values of life. Those who have particular wants and desires are thereby enabled to get the fulfilment of them by the grace of Lalitāmbikā. It cleanses one of sins, gives protection from enemies and from all kinds of dangers including the effects of black magic, cures serious ailments, bestows prosperity and progeny, endows one with the power of attracting others and exercising control over them, and enhances one's literary and poetic aptitudes. It is finally said that one who recites this Sahasranāma out of pure devotion to the Divine Mother, without any desire for worldly fulfilments, will attain the knowledge of Brahman and release from involvement in the cycle of births and deaths (Samsāra).

A critical person may doubt whether all these hyperbolic attainments mentioned in the Phala-Śruti (the panegyric of accruing benefits) are really attained. That will depend on one's unwavering faith and devotion. Besides, such declarations alone can attract the materially – minded man to the path of devotion.

EDITOR

KEY TO TRANSLITERATION AND PRONUNCIATION

		Sounds like			*Sounds like*
अ	a	o in son	ठ	th	th in ant-hill
आ	ā	a in master	ड	ḍ	d in den
इ	i	i in if	ढ	ḍh	dh in godhood
ई	ī	ee in feel	ण	ṇ	n in under
उ	u	u in full	त	t	t in French
ऊ	ū	oo in boot	थ	th	th in thumb
ऋ	ṛ	somewhat between r an ri	द	d	th in then
			ध	dh	then in breathe
ए	e	ay in May	न	n	n in not
ऐ	ai	y in my	प	p	p in pen
ओ	o	o in oh	फ	ph	ph in loop-hole
औ	au	ow in now	ब	b	b in bag
क	k	k in keen	भ	bh	bh in abhor
ख	kh	ckh in blockhead	म	m	m in mother
ग	g	g (hard) in go	य	y	y in yard
घ	gh	gh in log-hut	र	r	r in run
ङ	ṅ	ng in singer	ल	l	l in luck
च	c	ch (not k) chain	व	v	v in avert
छ	ch	chh in catch him	श	ś	sh in reich (German)
ज	j	j in judge	ष	ṣ	sh in show
झ	jh	dgeh in hedgehog	स	s	s in sun
ञ	ñ	n (somewhat) as in French	ह	h	in hot
			ं	ṁ	m in sum
ट	ṭ	t tn ten	:	ḥ	h in half

INTRODUCTION

By Prof.D.S.Sarma

I

The *Lalitāsahasranāma* is a sequel to the *Lalitopākhyāna* which forms part of the *Brahmāṇḍa Purāṇa.* It consists of three chapters. The first is only introductory, the second gives the thousand names of the great Goddess Lalitā and the third contains the usual *phalaśruti.*

In the introductory chapter Agastya, who has been listening to the account of the deeds of the Goddess given by Hayagrīva, as set forth in the *Lalitopākhyāna,* asks the latter why he did not include in his narrative the thousand names of the Goddess . He says:—

"You have narrated to me the most wonderful history of Lalitā Devī. You have narrated in detail the birth of the Mother, then her coronation, and then her slaying of the demon Bhaṇḍa. You have described Śrīpura in all its glory and also the greatness of the Pañcadaśī mantra...But you have not told me the thousand names of Lalitā Devī. Have you forgotten to do so or have you deliberately refrained? Or am I unworthy of hearing the names?"

Thus questioned, Hayagrīva replied, "I did not tell you, because I thought it was a secret. Now that you have asked me with devotion, I will impart it to you." And then he gave him the thousand names, saying that they had been composed by the Goddesses of speech at the express command of Lalitā Parameśvarī Herself.

II

The story of Lalitā to which the *Lalitāsahasranāma* thus refers is briefly as follows:—

When Manmatha, the god of love, was reduced to ashes by Śiva opening his third eye, the ashes were collected by Citrakarman, one of Śiva's attendants, and used for drawing the figure of a man. Śiva glanced at the figure and at once it leaped into life and became a living person. The artist now advised the person he thus created to pray to Śiva and repeat the Śata-Rudrīya. The person did so and Śiva was pleased and blessed him with the overlordship of the world for sixty thousand years. On hearing this, Brahmā cried in dismay, "Bhaṇḍ, Bhaṇḍ," and so the person came to have the name Bhaṇḍa. When Bhaṇḍa grew up, he became a great Asura and established his capital in Śoṇitapura. He oppresssed the gods and made life intolerable for them. Thereupon Nārada advised Indra, the king of the gods, to do penance and seek the help of Parā Śakti. Indra, accordingly, performed a great sacrifice, and out of the sacrificial fire there arose a great Cakra and, in the midst of it, was the lovely figure of the Devī who embodied[1] the spirit of the Trimūrti. The gods praised her and she promised to vanquish their enemy Bhaṇḍāsura. But Brahmā said that no person who remained single was fit for sovereignty according to the scriptures and exhorted her to choose a suitable mate. The gods commended the proposal and assured her that her independence would in no way suffer by her marriage. Then the Goddess consented and threw up a garland. It fell round the neck of Śiva who had assumed the lovely form of Kāmeśvara. The marriage of the beautiful couple was celebrated by the gods with great pomp and Lalitā became Kāmeśvarī and was crowned along with her husband. After the gods had left, the Goddess set out to fulfil her mission with an army of Śaktis well equipped with chariots, elephants and horses. The battle between her and the demon raged for four days and at last Bhaṇḍa was killed with all his kinsmen and followers, and his capital was razed to the ground. The gods praised the Goddess and requested her to take pity on Ratī, the wife of Manmatha who had been burnt to death by Śiva. She consented and revived the god of love and then went and settled down at Śrīnagara. This city was built for her by both Viśvakarma and Maya on one of the peaks of Mount Meru. An elaborate description of it is given in the Purāna. In the midst of this wonderful

---

[1] Brahma-Viṣṇu-Śivātmikām.

city is a palace built of precious Cintāmaṇi stones and in the centre of the palace is the seat of the Devī. On a jewelled cot, the legs of which are formed by Brahmā, Viṣṇu, Īśvara and Maheśvara and the coverlet by Sadāśiva, the great Goddess Śrī Lalitā Devī sits in the lap of her husband, Kāmeśvara. The Śrīcakra is, besides other things, a diagrammatic representation of the Goddess and her capital Śrīpura. Devotees of the Goddess are therefore exhorted to worship the Śrīcakra, perform japam with the Pañcadaśākṣarī mantra which forms the subtle body of the Devī and repeat this litany of a thousand names, which was composed by the Goddesses of speech at the express command of Śrī Lalitā Paramesvarī herself.

III

The Avatār of the Bhagavad Gītā says in a well-known verse, "Howsoever men approach me, even so do I accept them." We may therefore approach God and call Him either father or mother. God is in truth beyond the distinctions of sex and even beyond personality, as we too often conceive it. The ineffable Absolute is endowed by us with the highest attributes we can think of, so as to bring it into relation with us and the world we live in. Accordingly, the distinction between the impersonal Brahman and the personal Iśvara is well recognised in our philosophy. The former is God as He is in Himself, the latter is God as He appears to us, when He is viewed through human spectacles. We may call these two views of God the scientific view and the spiritual view respectively. The impersonal Absolute, when viewed through the human mind, becomes a personal God. And this personal God in His capacity as creator becomes Brahmā, as protector becomes Viṣṇu and as destroyer becomes Rudra. And, lastly, when as protector He comes down and takes a human form to save mankind from evil, He becomes an Avatār. Thus we try to bridge the yawning gulf between the Supreme Spirit and the spirit of man.

When the Absolute is thus brought into relation with us and the world we live in, we have inevitably to think of it as an active power. Hence the distinction that we draw between the quiescent Brahman and the active Iśvara. In Śakta theology, this distinction is transferred to Śiva and Śakti. Śiva corresponds to the inactive Brahman and Śakti corresponds to the active Iśvara. And, as the word 'Śakti' is of feminine gender in Sanskrit, the personification results in a Goddess. Śiva is Śakti, and Śakti is Śiva, as Brahman is Iśvara and Iśvara is Brahman. In fact, they are only two different aspects of the same Reality. They are the static and the dynamic aspects of the same Spirit. They are as inseparable as fire and heat or sun and sunshine. But Śakti, the dynamic aspect of the Reality, is more important to us, as we are caught up in this dynamic universe of created beings and have in us an urge to transcend our present state.

If Iśvara, as we said above, is a spiritual conception of the Absolute, Iśvarī or Śakti or Devī is certainly an equally valid one. And, as we generally fear our fathers and love our mothers, the concept of a mother-Goddess appeals more to our hearts than that of a father-god. Also, in the representation of a female deity, there is more scope for grace and beauty, and hence for greater poetry and art. Accordingly in the *Lalitāsahasranāma*, which is a *stotra* addressed to a Goddess ,we see poetry and romance, religion and philosophy, occultism and psychology vying with one another in coining names for the deity. The author has embodied in this litany not only the Purāṇic story of Lalitā and her fight with the demon Bhaṇḍa, but also the philosophy and the ritual of Śrī Vidyā. The most striking feature of the hymn is the perfect balance it maintains between its pure poetry and its technical theology by means of the genuine religious spirit which runs through it. In dealing with his subject-matter, the author had to avoid two pitfalls. On the one hand, there was the danger of his litany becoming a purely secular poem like the Āgamani songs addressed to the Goddess by the Bengali poets of a later day, and, on the other, there was the danger of the hymn becoming a mere exposition of a system of theology like the Tantras of an earlier day. And he has succeeded in avoiding both. His poetry never ceases to be religious and his philosophy seldom becomes merely technical. His admiration for the dazzling beauty of the Goddess and his comprehension of all that she stands for in the hearts of men go up in fine jets of poetry, even while he is expounding abstract philosophy or complex ritual. Consequently, the Goddess in this hymn neither vanishes into the thin air of a mere idea, nor comes down to the earth as a purely human figure. She remains a Goddess of transcendent beauty, leading a host of divinities against the forces of evil. She is not a cold virgin, but a young wife passionately fond of her husband—Kāmeśvara. She is also a mother who loves her children and takes pride in their exploits. She is ever young, ever rosy like the morning sun, and the jewels she wears rival the stars in their splendour. Her breath has the perfume of camphor, her voice is sweeter than the Vīṇa of Sarasvatī, and her person is fragrant with the scent of sandal. She is passionately fond of flowers—Campaka, Asoka, Punnāga and others and constantly wears them in her hair. She is herself a flower, says the poet. She shines like a china rose or like a pomegranate flower or a Bandhūka blossom. But she is more fond of the flowers of the spirit *(caitanya kusuma priyā)*. She is fond of poetry, of dancing and music and the chanting of the Veda. She is, in fact, the home of all arts, the treasure-house of all *rasas.* She is the essence of all scriptures as well. She is the priceless pearl, says the poet, hidden in the depths of all scriptures. The Vedas bow to her and take the dust of her feet on their heads, for, is she not their mother? And what do the Upaniṣads proclaim? They proclaim only her glory. She is worshipped by the highest gods in heaven and yet she is accessible to all—even to the child and the peasant. Her grace is easily won, for her mercy demands no merit on our part. She is the light that dispels the darkness of our hearts. She is the rain of nectar that falls on the parched soil of our earthly existence. She is the wind that drives away all our misfortunes. She is the thunderbolt that cleaves asunder the mountains of human ills. She is a *Kalpataru* and a *Kāmadhenu* to all her worshippers. At the same time, she is the ultimate Reality—above all *tattvas* and categories of thought, above all dualisms—the one indivisible Spirit, without qualities, without parts—ever free, ever pure—formless and timeless—and without a cause, without a lapse and without a limit.

IV

Such a magnificent conception of the Goddess is, of course, the result of a long process of evolution, beginning probably with a crude tribal deity in the dim pre-historic past. There are some critics who, in judging religions and cults other than their own, invariably point the finger of scorn at their humble, undignified origins and ignore their later developments. We should judge a tree by its fruits, not by its roots. The fruit may be sweet and fragrant, while the roots may be buried in stinking soil and manure. It is quite probable that in the present case, as critics point out, not one but many tribal deities worshipped in different places and at different times have been fused together in the course of ages and made into a single Deity and then subjected to all the refining influences of poetry, religion and philosophy and, not the least of all, to the wonderful charm and grace of Indian womanhood. Speaking of the women of India, Mrs.Besant once said in her own characteristic way, "Fairer flowers never grew on this earth." It is the idealization of these flowers of the earth that gives us this heavenly flower of Devī Lalitā of transcendent beauty and fragrance. The Lalitās, the Sītās and the Sāvitrīs of poetry could not have come into being, had not their creators been inspired by the Lalitās, the Sītās and the Sāvitrīs in real life. There is no doubt that the poet of the *Lalitāsahasranāma* has drawn as much from the life around him as from tradition and legend, and religion and philosophy. We should remember that he lived in a country which, even amidst the many crudities of its social life, developed the doctrine that every woman is an incarnation of the Goddess and may be actually worshipped in her place—a doctrine that should give rise in the hearts of men to far purer feelings and sentiments than the code of chivalry that prevailed in mediaeval Europe. Woodroffe quotes from one of the Tantras which says, "Whosoever has seen the feet of woman, let him worship them as those of his guru." *(Strīṇām pādatalam dṛṣṭvā guruvad-bhāvayet sadā—Kubjikā Tantra).*

V

The process of evolution mentioned above was similar to that earlier process by which the Vedic gods gave place in later times to the supreme God of a monotheistic faith—a Viṣṇu or a Śiva. And, first of all, just as there were no hard and fast lines between one Vedic god and another, each of the gods fading off into the others, so there were no hard and fast lines between one Goddess and another. The famous Vedic dictum, Ekam Sat, viprā bahudhā vadanti—(The Reality is one, the wise speak of it in different ways)— applied as much to the later Goddesses as to the earlier gods. Also, just as Viṣṇu is said to have descended several times to punish the wicked Rākṣasas, a Hiraṇyakaśipu, a Rāvaṇa or a Śiśupāla, so in the parallel development of the Devī, we have several of her forms arising to quell the demons of the day—Caṇḍī arising to quell Mahiṣāsura, Kālī coming to kill Caṇḍa and Muṇḍa, and Lalitā rising out of the sacrificial fire to slay Bhaṇḍa and his sons. And, closely parallel to the famous Gītā passage in which the Bhagavān explains why He comes down as an Avatār from age to age, we have the following passage in the *Devī Māhātmya:*

"Whenever there is trouble of this kind caused by the Dānavas, at each such time I shall incarnate myself and accomplish the destruction of the enemy."

Thus in the history of our religion there have arisen two types of monotheism—one centring round a supreme God and another round a supreme Goddess, both of whom are admittedly only symbols of the impersonal Absolute.

VI

In the early Vedic literature we have no supreme Goddess any more than a supreme God. There were a number of Goddesses like Uṣas, Rātri, Vāk, Prithivī and Sarasvatī, and a number of consorts of gods, like Indrāṇī, Varuṇānī, etc. But all of them occupy a very subordinate position. However, before the end of the Vedic period we see signs of the emergence of a supreme Goddess as well as of a supreme God. Just as Viṣṇu rises in importance by assimilating to himself the traits of Indra, Sūrya and Varuṇa, so does the consort of Rudra by assimilating to herself the traits of the other

Goddesses, especially Vāk. For instance, in a passage in the Taittirīya Āraṇyaka she is referred to by three different names - Kātyāyanī, Kanyākumārī and Durgā. In the Kena Upaniṣad she is identified with Umā Haimavatī, who symbolizes Brahma-vidyā. And two other names which afterwards become associated with her, *viz.*, Kalī and Karālī, occur in the Muṇḍaka Upaniṣad where they denote two tongues of fire. This process of syncretism which begins in the Vedic period itself continues in the Epic period on a much larger scale, till at last a Devī-worshipping sect is formed, equal in status to the worshippers of Viṣṇu and Śiva, by the beginning of the Purāṇic period. There are two hymns in the Mahābhārata which illustrate the process. They are both addressed to Durgā. One is by Yudhiṣṭhira just before the Paṇḍavas enter the kingdom of Virāṭa, and another by Arjuna on the battlefield of Kurukṣetra just before the Bhagavad Gītā episode. Both are evidently later interpolations, for they are not found in the best South Indian manuscripts. However, they afford interesting study. In the earlier hymn we are told that the Goddess is a virgin observing a vow of chastity. Her constant abode is on the Vindhya mountains. She is called Durgā, Kālī and Mahiṣāsura-nāśinī. She takes delight in wine and meat and sacrificial victims. She is identified, all the same, with Vidyā, Siddhi, Kānti, etc. And, in the introduction to the hymn, she is described as the child of Yaśodā and the sister of Kṛṣṇa—the one who ascended the skies when dashed by Kamsa on the stony ground. The hymn to the Goddess by Arjuna is more interesting. Curiously enough, it is at the instance of Kṛṣṇa himself that Arjuṇa descends from his chariot and prays to Durgā for success in battle. The Goddess appears before him and assures him of victory. One of the noteworthy features of the hymn is the number of names by which the Goddess is addressed. She is called Kumārī, Kāpālī, Kapilā, Bhadrakālī, Mahākālī, Caṇḍī, Kātyāyanī, Karālī, Kausikī, Umā, Śākambharī, Mohinī, Māyā, etc. Here again she is described as the sister of Kṛṣṇa and as having been born in the cowherd family of Nanda. She is adorned with various jewels and armed with spear and sword and shield. She delights in battle and thirsts for the blood of Mahiṣa. She lives in inaccessible places, in places full of fears and difficulties as well as in *caityas* and the abodes of her devotees. She dwells in the nether regions also and conquers the demons in battle. Her virginity is not mentioned. On the other hand, she is described as the mother of Skanda. She is the mother of the Vedas as well, and she is hailed as Brahma-vidyā among Vidyās.

In the Viṣṇu-purāṇa there is, again, an interesting passage on the Goddess. Viṣṇu, while giving instructions to his Yoga-nidrā as to what she should do in connection with the birth of Kṛṣṇa, says:

"Those who shall reverently invoke you morning and evening and praise and call you Āryā, Durgā, Vedagarbhā, Ambikā, Bhadrā, Bhadrakālikā, Kṣemī or Kṣemaṅkarī shall receive by my grace whatever they desire. And pleased with their offerings of wine and flesh and various other kinds you shall grant the prayers of mankind. By my favour, all men shall have perpetual faith in you. Assured of this, go, Goddess, and carry out my orders".

Finally, there is a hymn in the Harivamṣa which throws some light again on the origins of the Goddess. Here too she is described as the sister of Krsna and as living in the Vindhya mountains and in all sorts of fearful places—caves, forests and groves—and as being greatly worshipped by savage tribes—Śabaras, Barbaras and Pulindas. But she is also described as the Savitṛ of the Vedas and hailed as the knower of Brahman and finally as supreme Brahman.

On these early hymns Bhandarkar makes the following comment in his book—*Vaishnavism, Saivism, etc:—*

"In the account here given it will be seen that there is one Goddess with a number of different names. But the critical eye will see that they are not merely names, but indicate different Goddesses who owed their conception to different historical conditions but who were afterwards identified with the one Goddess by the usual mental habit of the Hindus".

The critical eye will see here something more than what the learned author has indicated. It will see not only the process of identification by which a host of tribal deities are brought under one supreme Goddess, but also another mental habit of the Hindus of those days—that of bringing all the cults and cultures of the land under the aegis of the Veda and the spiritualizing influence of the Vedanta philosophy, while allowing them to retain a large measure of their individuality. For we find that the tribal deity of mountain fastnesses, who is fond of flesh and wine and the sacrificial victims offered by the tribesmen, is here already being hailed as the mother of the Vedas and the presiding deity of Brahma-vidyā and even being identified with Brahman. These are the germs which develop later into the mighty theophanies of the *Devi-Māhātmya* and the *Lalitāsahasranāma*.And, as this development proceeds apace, the mountain fastnesses, the inaccessible places, the sacrificial victims and the spirituous liquors of the early hymns shrink into mere specks on a vast flood of spirituality. For instance, miles away as the *Lalitā* is from these odes, we still hear distinct echoes of them in its thousand names. We are still told that the Goddess lives in the Vindhya mountains *(Vindhyācala-nivāsinī)* that she is fond of mead *(kādambarī-priyā)* and that she even becomes intoxicated *(vāruṇī-mada-vihvalā, mādhvī-pānālasā)*. But we hardly remember these merely traditional epithets in the flood of the new subject-matter regarding the marvellous beauty of the Goddess, her heroic fight with the forces of evil, her vast and varied powers and her extensive dominion in the hearts of men. To take one example, while the early hymns describe her as living in dreary deserts *(kāntāra-vāsinī)*, the *Lalitā* describes her as the swan that swims in the hearts of saints *(muni - mānasa - haṁsikā)*.

VII

A distinct stage in the process of development is represented by the famous *Caṇḍī-Māhātmya* in the Mārkaṇḍeya Purāṇa, which describes the Devī's fight with Mahiṣāsura and the other demons, Śumbha and Niśumbha. The very story of her birth is significant of the new developments. There was once a long war between the gods and the demons. The former were headed by Indra and the latter by Mahiṣa. The gods were vanquished and Mahiṣa became supreme. The vanquished gods went to Viṣṇu and Śiva and told them of their discomfiture. When Viṣṇu and Śiva heard their plaints they became very angry and there issued from their mouths a great *tejas.* And from the bodies of the other gods also there went forth at the same time great energies. All these energies gathered together and assumed a female form. The gods were pleased and each of them gave her a weapon or an ornament. Accepting these gifts, the Goddess mounted the lion which had been presented to her by Himavat and uttered a loud roar as a challenge to the enemy. The demons heard the roar and rushed to the place headed by Mahiṣa. Then began a fierce battle between the Goddess and her enemies "in which every region of the sky was illumined with weapons, and arms were hurled in abundance".

At last the Goddess, who had fortified herself with a cup of wine, leapt on the Asura and kicked him on the neck with her foot, struck him with her spear and cut off his head with her sword. This detail of the Devī kicking the demon half-dead with her foot is important, for almost the whole of *Candī-śataka* of Bāṇa is based on it. Bāṇa's poem is an ode more to the foot of the Goddess than to the Goddess herself. After Mahiṣa was slain, the gods and ṛiṣis assembled together and sang paeans of praise and thanksgiving for their deliverance. They asked a boon of the Goddess that, whenever they called on her for help in similar difficulties, she should come to their rescue. "Be it so", said the Goddess and vanished from their sight.

Then the narrative proceeds to describe how on another occasion the gods prayed to her for help against Śumbha and Niśumbha who had conquered them and driven them from heaven. While they were thus praying on the Himalayas, Pārvatī came there to bathe in the Ganges and asked them, "Whom are you praying to?" At once from her own body issued forth Ambikā and said, "For me is this hymn uttered by the gods who have been routed by Śumbha and Niśumbha." This new Goddess was surpassingly beautiful. She illumined the whole sky with her lustre, and reports of her presence were taken to the two demons by their servants, Caṇḍa and Muṇḍa. Śumbha thereupon sent a message to her, offering her his hand in marriage. The Goddess replied that she had taken a vow that she would marry only that hero who could vanquish her in an open fight. So if Śumbha wanted to marry her, he should come at once and fight with her. This challenge was joyfully accepted by the demon and the fight began. The battle on this occasion was much more prolonged and fierce than the battle with Mahiṣa. At one stage of it, the Goddess grew so dark with rage that out of her forehead issued forth Kālī with a terrible form, clad in a tiger skin and wearing a garland of skulls and lolling out her tongue for the blood of the enemy. The fight now becomes most ghastly. Kālī roams about on the battlefield crushing the demons or devouring them or drinking the blood of the slain. She destroys Caṇḍa and Muṇḍa and is rewarded by Ambikā with the title of Cāmuṇḍā. After her work is over, Kālī retires again into the body of Caṇḍī, who thereafter single-handed despatches the two leaders—Śumbha and Niśumbha, and the fight comes to a close. The gods sing again a hymn of thanksgiving, and the Goddess vanishes after promising that she will take birth again and again for vanquishing the wicked demons in the future ages.

VIII

In the course of this narrative we find four hymns to the Goddess, which show a great advance from the early hymns we have already considered. First of all, the very origin of the Goddess, as we said above, is significant. It indicates that Caṇḍī is not simply a Goddess with many names, but that she is the very essence of all the gods, including Brahmā, Viṣṇu and Śiva. Secondly, she is now represented as having two sets of forms—a set of gentle forms and a set of terrible forms. In the gentle form she is surpassingly beautiful and in the terrible form she is surpassingly fearful. Thirdly, it is interesting to notice that, while in the early hymns the name Durgā is explained as one who rescues men from dangers and difficulties ,it is explained here as one who helps men to cross the difficult ocean of existence. It is also stressed that the Devī can give prosperity on earth and happiness in heaven and also emancipation from samsāra. Fourthly, great emphasis is laid on her immanence. In one of the hymns here, there are more than twenty ślokas beginning with the words *yā devī sarvabhūteṣu* and saying that the Goddess is present in all creatures as consciousness, as power, as intellect, as memory, as desire and so on. And, finally, equally great emphasis is laid on her connection with Viṣṇu. She is not only called Viṣṇumāyā and hailed as the sister of Kṛṣṇa as in the early hymns, but is also addressed as Nārāyaṇī in seventeen ślokas and identified with his śakti which had manifested itself in the Avatārs. She is likewise represented as being the Śakti of Brahmā, Maheśvara, Kumāra and Indra. Thus we have here the beginnings of the doctrine of Śakti which afterwards led to astonishing developments in the worship of the Goddess.

IX

The Devī cult enters on a new stage in the period which saw the rise of Tāntric literature in our country. Such works as the *Lalitāsahasranāma,* the *Devī Bhāgavata* and the *Saundaryalaharī* and the later *Śākta Upaniṣads* as well as the Tantras themselves represent this stage of development. The period may be said to begin from the seventh century A.D. The Tantras of the Śakti-worshippers, which are generally in the form of dialogues between Śiva and Śakti, are treatises which, unlike the older Purāṇas, are wholly devoted to the philosophy and the ritual of the cult. Strictly speaking, a Tantra, according to the definitions given, should consists of (1) jñāna, *i.e.,* philosophical doctrines; (2) yoga, i.e., instructions regarding meditation; (3) kriyā, i.e., instructions regarding ritual; (4) caryā, i.e., instructions regarding conduct and social duties. But very few of the sixty-four Tantras known to us strictly observe this regulation. The Tantras are essentially sādhana śāstras. Their aim is severely practical. They generally accept the philosophy of the Advaita Vedāntā and suggest ways and means of reaching the goal of that philosophy, *viz.,*self-realization. However, some of the modifications they introduce into the Vedāntic theories of the ultimate Reality and of the process of creation lead to striking innovations in the worship of the Devī.

As in the Advaita, we have in the Tāntric philosophy also one ultimate Reality called here Parama Śiva, who is again conceived of as being both niṣkala and sakala (partless whole and with parts). And, as in the Advaita, the world is considered a lesser reality in a sense; for it owes its existence to the association of Brahman with Māyā or, to use the Tāntric terms, Śiva with Śakti. But, while Māyā in the Advaita is *anirvacanīya* or that which cannot be described to be either true or false, Śakti in the

Tāntric philosophy possesses as much reality as Śiva: In fact, the two are identical. Thus, while the changes in the world are less real in the sense that they are only the temporary modifications of the same identity, viz., Śiva-Śakti, they are real in the sense that they are the modifications of an entity which is *entirely* real. The Advaita says there is no real change, but only the appearance of it. The Tantra, on the other hand, says that the ultimate Reality is immutable in one aspect, but undergoes a real evolution in another aspect. The Advaita effects its synthesis by its doctrine of different levels of reality, but the Tantra does it by its doctrine of unity in duality and duality in unity. According to the Tantra, the ultimate Reality is neither wholly static nor wholly dynamic. It is both. For, while Śiva is the *prakāśa* aspect of the Reality—that is, pure self - illumining thought, impersonal, inactive and devoid of any relativity, Śakti is the *vimarśa*[1] aspect of the same Reality—that is, the inherent activity of thought. Śiva is pure consciousness, Śakti is the formative energy of that consciousness. That which appears as thought in one aspect appears as activity in another. Śakti is the power latent in pure unrelated consciousness. It is the Absolute personified. It is consciousness developing subject - object relationship, which gives rise to the world of

[1] 'Vimarśa' is the same as the Vedāntic 'Ikṣaṇa'.

distinctions and changes. It is these ideas of Śāktā philosophy that are expressed in the *Lalitāsahasranāma* through the names—*Śiva - śakty - aikyarūpiṇī, Cideka - rasa - rūpiṇī, Śiva - mūrtiḥ, Śivā, Svaprakāśā, Vimaraśa - rūpiṇī,* etc.

X

In its account of the evolution of the world from Śivā-Śakti, the Tantra accepts the twenty-four tattvas or categories of the Sānkhya system from Prakṛti down to the Mahābhūtas and adds twelve more, taking them from the Śaiva system with some modifications, and makes them thirty-six. And these are divided into three groups—(1) five pure tattvas; (2) seven partly pure and partly impure tattvas and (3) the twenty-four impure tattvas as in the Sānkhya. The first group consists of (a) Śiva, (b) Śakti, (c) Nāda, (d) Bindu and (e) Śuddha-Vidyā; and it is here that we have the Tāntric modifications, for, in the Śaiva system, corresponding to these, we have (a) Śiva, (b) Śakti, (c) Sadāśiva (d) Iśvara and (e) Śuddha-vidyā. In the Tāntric scheme the first two tattvas *viz.,* Śiva-tattva and Śakti-tattva are really one. As we have already said, the former is the static and the latter the dynamic aspect of the ultimate Reality. Then we come to Nāda and Bindu. Nāda here does not mean sound, and Bindu does not mean a drop. In the philosophy of the Tantra they have become technical words denoting successive moments in creation. Nāda denotes the thrill of the first impulse towards creation, and Bindu, which means a point , symbolizes the infinite potentialities of the universe about to be unfolded. The writers of the Tantra often compare it to a grain of gram (caṇaka) which within its husk contains a double seed in undivided union, from which the sprout will rise and grow into a plant. The seeds are, of course, Śiva and Śakti. The former is Prakāśa and the latter Vimarśa, as explained above. Prakāśa passes into Vimarśa and is reflected back into itself and becomes self-conscious. Thought can know itself only when it is reflected in action. And when it is so reflected it becomes individualized. Thus the original Bindu, called Parābindu or Mahābindu becomes differentiated into three—the śvetabindu, the point of pure thought; the raktabindu or the point of activity which acts as a reflector and the miśrabindu, the point of the return of thought through action, resulting in the union of both under the principle of individuality. The three differentiated bindus are sometimes represented by a triangle. They are together called Kāmakalā. Here Kāma, according to one interpretation, means both Kāmeśvara and Kāmesvarī, and Kalā is their manifestation. This threefold aspect of Bindu is also spoken of as Jñānaśakti, Kriyāśakti and Icchāśakti, and figuratively described as Tripura-sundarī. The rest of the tattvas are the same as in the Śaiva and Sānkhya systems and call for no comment. It is in accordance with this theory of creation that the author of the *Lalitā* calls the Goddess *Nādarūpā, Nādarūpiṇī, Bindumaṇḍala - vāsinī, Baindavāsanā, Kāma - kalā - rūpā, Śrīmattripura - sundarī, Tattvāsana, Tattvamayī, Icchā - śakti jñānaśakti - kriyāśakti - svarūpiṇī.,* etc.

XI

Just as the Tāntric philosophy adapted for its own purpose some of the ideas of the Vedānta, Sānkhya and Śaiva systems, so also it laid the Mimāmsā and Yoga systems under contribution. The Mimāmsakas believed that both śabda and artha—words and their meanings—are eternal. The denotation of a word, according to them, did not depend on any human convention, but belonged to the nature of the word itself. The word is eternal and therefore its denotation is also eternal. Also, the word is not in any way different from the letters composing it, though when it is pronounced we hear only a unity of sounds. The Mīmāmsakas, however, believed that both śabda and artha were inanimate. The Tantra accepted the Mīmāmsakas' theory of the eternality of śabda and artha, but asserted that they were as much the embodiments of Śiva-Śakti as the universe itself. In fact, they called their Parābindu Śabdārtha-Brahman instead of mere Śabda-Brahman. For it was the source of both words and things. Śabda as well as artha—words as well as objects—are manifestations of Śakti. And, as śabda was of the nature of the varṇas composing it, the Tantra affirmed that the creative force of the universe resided in all the letters of the alphabet. The different letters symbolized the different functions of that creative force, and their totality was designated mātṛikā or the Mother in miniature. Thus we arrive at the famous doctrine that a mantra is not a mere combination of sounds, but is the subtle form of the presiding Devatā herself, and that the object of one's meditation on the mantra is to identify oneself with the Devatā of the mantra. Again, just as pure thought has to pass through several stages before it becomes a concrete creative force, so it was believed that sound has to pass through several stages before it is actually heard by the ear. These stages were called *parā, paśyantī, madhyamā* and *vaikharī,* and these were believed to be as much the phases of the divine Śakti as the stages in the evolution of the universe. This theory of the eternality of śabda and artha, which the Tantra had borrowed from the Mīmāmsā and transformed through its own vital doctrine of Śakti, has had a remarkable development in our mantra-śāstra and has produced marvellous results in practice.

The most celebrated mantra connected with the worship of the Devī is the Pañcadaśākṣarī mantra. As its name indicates, it consists of fifteen syllables divided into three kūṭas or sections, known as Vagbhava-kūṭa presided over by Agni, Kāmarāja-kūṭa presided over by Sūrya and Śakti-kūṭa presided over by Soma. The mantra, it cannot be too often repeated, is not a mere formula. It is the Devī herself in her subtle form. The Pañcadaśākṣarī mantra may be called the Gāyatrī of the Śāktas. In his book *Varivasyārahasyam*, Bhāskararāya, the celebrated commentator on the *Lalitāsahasranāma*,takes pains to point out that this mantra could, indeed, be interpreted in fifteen different ways, so as to establish its identity with the Gāyatrī, its identity with the Devī, its identity with the Tattvas, its identity with Śri Cakra and so on. And just as the Gāyatrī, which is usually said to contain three feet (tripadā), has also a fourth foot, which is kept secret and communicated only to a few adepts, so the fifteen syllabled mantra has also a sixteenth syllable which is kept secret. When this sixteenth syllable is also taken into consideration the mantra is called ṣoḍaśākṣarī mantra. With this background in view we are now in a position to understand in the *Lalitāsahasranāma* the significance of names like *mātṛikā - varṇa - rūpinī; pañcāśat - pīṭha - rūpiṇī, sarvaṁantra - svarūpiṇī* and the series—*parā, paśyantī, madhyamā, vaikharī - rūpā.*

The syllables of the Pancadaśākṣarī mantra are not given in the *Sahasranāma* either directly or indirectly, but the three kūṭas of it are mentioned and identified with the face, the trunk and the limbs of the Goddess in the following names:—

śrīmad - vāgbhava - kūṭaika - svarūpa - mukha - paṅkajā, kaṇṭhādhaḥ - kaṭiparyanta - madhyakūṭa - svarūpiṇī, śakti - kūṭaikatāpanna - kaṭydhobhāga - dhāriṇi, mūla - mantrātmikā, mūla - kūṭa - traya - kalebarā, śrīṣodaśākṣarī - vidyā, trikūṭā, etc.

It may be observed, by the way, that while the *Lalitāsahasranāma* does not give the syllables of the Pañcadaśākṣarī, the *Lalitātriśatī,* which contains only three hundred names, has twenty names beginning with each of the syllables and thus gives the mantra indirectly.

XII

The creative world-process, according to the Tāntric philosophy, is seen not only in the production of articulate speech but also in the organization of the human body. That man is an epitome of the universe, that the microcosm is an exact parallel to the macrocosm, that conditions are the same in both *piṇḍa* and *brahmāṇḍa* is a very ancient idea. It had found expression in various ways in the Upaniṣads. The Tantra took up this idea and made it the basis of an elaborate system of sādhana. The creative force of the universe which was supposed to dwell in the letters of the alphabet was also supposed to dwell in the nerve-centres of the human system. In fact, the creation of the exterior world-order, the production of articulate speech and the organization of the human body with its nerve-centres are, according to the Tantra, the manifestations of the same primordial Śakti. The divine power dwells as surely in the human body as it dwells in the sounds of speech and in the elements of the universe. The Goddess is in us as surely as she is in the worlds she has created and in the mantras she has revealed. So one way of realizing her is to concentrate our attention on the nerve-plexuses, or cakras, as they are called, in our system, and develop the divine power latent in every one of us.

These cakras are described as so many symbolic lotuses, each with its own fixed number of petals, its own presiding Śaktis and its own association with various (1) tattvas, (2) varṇaṣ and (3) bhāvas (or elements, letters and emotions)[1] . The most important of these lotuses are mulādhāra, svādhiṣṭhāna, maṇipūra, anāhata, viśuddha and ājñā. They are generally divided into three groups:

---

[1] There is a difference of opinion about the association of tattvas. Some associate maṇipūra with fire, others with water. The author of *Ṣat - cakra - nirūpaṇa* holds the former view, while the author of the *Saundarya - laharī* holds the latter view.

(1) Mulādhāra, which is at the end of the spinal column in the pelvic region, and Svādhiṣṭhāna, which is a little above the genitals, form what is known as Agnikhaṇḍa. Above this group is a granthi or knot known as Brahma-granthi.

(2) Maṇipūra, which is near the navel, and Anāhata, which is near the heart, form what is known as Sūrya-khaṇḍa, and above them is the knot, Viṣṇugranthi.

(3) Viśuddha, which is near the throat, and Ājñā, which is between the eye-brows, form what is known as Candra-khaṇḍa, and above them is the knot Rudragranthi. Above these six important cakras is the Sahasrāra in the head. As its name indicates, it is a lotus of a thousand petals. It is the seat of Śiva-Śakti.

According to the yoga system of philosophy, when the mind is concentrated on any tattva, say, earth, water, fire or air, the sādhaka becomes one with it and is able to rise through its own inner power to higher and higher tattvas, till he gains liberation from Prakṛiti itself. The Tantra adopts this principle of discipline and teaches that the sādhaka should by appropriate means rouse the Kuṇḍalinī Śakti which lies coiled in him like a serpent in the mulādhāra and make it go up from one cakra to another—that is, from one tattva to another—piercing the three granthis mentioned above, till she reaches the sahasrāra and becomes united with Śiva there. The sādhaka thus attains self-realization, which is the goal of the whole sādhana.[1]

It should be noted here that, though we call these cakras nerve-centres, they are really psychological levels and not physiological plexuses, for they are unknown to modern anatomy or physiology. So what we have to understand by the practice of Kuṇḍalinī-yoga, is that the sādhaka, by means of concentration of mind, has to rise from one level of consciousness to another passing through one spiritual crisis after another—for that is the meaning of a Granthi—till he reaches the level of universal consciousness. Thus, it will be observed, the doctrine of ṣat-cakra-bheda is parallel to that of the upāsana of the Pañcadaśākṣarī mantra, the three khaṇḍas of the former corresponding to the three kūṭas of the latter.

It is necessary for us to know these details of the Kuṇḍalinī yoga for understanding a good number of names in the *Lalitā,* as the author deals rather extensively with this subject. For instance, the names from No.99 to No.110 refer to the cakras and the Granthis mentioned above. They are as follows:—

[1] "This eternal union of the Jīva and Paramātman in the Sahasrāra is known as going into the seventh plane." (Sri Ramakrishna.)

*mulādhāraika-nilayā, brahma-granthi-vibhedinī, maṇipūrantā-ruditā, viṣṇu-granthi-vibhedinī, ājñā-cakrānt'arālasthā, rudra-granthi-vibhedinī, sahasrā-rāmbujā- rūḍhā, sudhāsārābhivarṣiṇī,*etc.

And, not satisfied with this, he devotes again about sixty names (No.475—No.534), giving a mass of rather tiresome details about the seven Śaktis—Ḍākinī, Rākiṇī, etc., dwelling in these seven lotuses, together with their forms, colours, tastes, weapons and attendants. And each of these Śaktis is supposed to be a form of the supreme Goddess herself.

XIII

The kind of symbolism by which the various aspects of the divine governance of the world are represented by means of deities with their appropriate lokas, vāhanas āyudhas etc., is, of course, very common in our Purāṇas; and our sculptural and pictorial arts are mainly based on it. Sometimes it is simply symbolism run mad. The Tantra, as we have seen, adopts the same method for representing the governance of the *inner world of man* and indicating the various psychological levels to be reached in his progress towards God. It goes further and employs diagrams called yantras for representing these Śaktis. It is but appropriate that a Śakti, which is of the nature of force or energy, should be represented by lines and curves and their combinations. For surely a diagram consisting of mere lines and points is a more spiritual symbol of a divinity than an anthropomorphic image of it in the round or a picture of it in colours. That is why the Tantra regards yantropāsana as being superior to the older pratīkopāsana. And the greatest of all yantras, according to it, is the famous Śrī Cakra, which is the central object of worship in Śrī Vidya.

The Śrī Cakra, again, like the Pañcadaśākṣarī mantra, is considered a form of the Goddess.[1] If the mantra is a revelation of the Mother in sounds, the yantra is a revelation of her in lines. And it is a symbol of the Devī not only in her true form as Śiva and Śakti in one, but also in her three phenomenal forms—the universe of mahābhūtas and the two miniature universes of the human body and the alphabet of articulate speech (varṇamālā).

The Śrī Cakra is that rather complicated diagram of interlocked triangles with which we are all more or less familiar. It consists of a circle with a Bindu at the centre. On the vertical diameter of this circle are arranged five triangles with their apexes pointing downwards and four triangles with their apexes pointing upwards. The former

---

[1] चक्रस्यापि महेश्या न भेदलेशोऽपि भाव्यते विबुधैः—

Kāmakalā-vilāsa.

are indicative of Śakti and the latter of Śiva and are called Śiva-yuvatis and Śrīkaṇṭhas respectively. The circle in which these nine triangles are interlocked is enclosed in two other concentric circles technically called lotuses. The first outer circle is a lotus of eight petals, and the second a lotus of sixteen petals. The circumference of the second is moreover marked not by one line, but by four lines close to one another. The whole figure is then enclosed in a quadrilateral the walls of which are formed of three parallel lines drawn close to one another. The quadrilateral is moreover provided with four openings—one at the centre of each side.

The diagram thus obtained is said to consist of nine parts technically called cakras. They are—according to Layakrama, ī.e., if we proceed from outside to the centre—as follows:—

(1) The three-lined quadrilateral called Bhūgṛha
(2) The sixteen-petalled lotus (ṣōḍaśa-dala-padma)
(3) The eight-petalled lotus (aṣṭa-dala-padma)
(4) The cakra of fourteen triangles (caturdaśāra)
(5) The cakra of ten outer triangles (bahir-daśāra)
(6) The cakra of ten inner triangles (antar-daśāra)
(7) The cakra of eight triangles (aṣṭa-koṇa)
(8) One inner triangle (trikoṇa)
(9) The central point (Bindu)

See illustration

—

There are technical names for all these parts and each part has its own colour. But it is unnecessary here to go into further details except to state that the central Bindu is called Sarvānandamaya and is coloured red. It represents the united *Kāmeśvara-Kāmeśvarī* called Tripura Sundarī or Lalitāmbikā.

Elaborate correspondences are worked out by writers on Śrī Cakra between its nine parts and (1) the tattvas of the universe (2) the varṇas of the alphabet, (3) the cakras of the human body and (4) even the tithis of the month and the days of the year. Moreover each part is supposed to be guarded by various Āvaraṇa-devatās or subordinate Śaktis having different functions. In the Bindu, for instance, there are fifteen Nityās surrounding the Devī. In the early stages of worship the sādhaka is taught to look upon these devatās presiding over the various parts of Śrī Cakra as separate deities, and later that all of them are only fragments of one primordial Śakti which created the universe and man and his speech and dwells in them, and, finally, that he himself is one with this Śakti.

Thus the Sri Cakra is a symbolic representation of all the fundamental principles of Tāntric philosophy. Hence its unique place in Tāntric worship. The *Lalitāsahasranāma* indicates this in the names—*śrīcakrarāja -nilayā, cakrarāja-niketanā, trikoṇagā and triko-ṇāntara-dīpikā.*

XIV

While the Upāsana of Pañcadaśākṣarī mantra, the practice of Kuṇḍalinī yoga and the pūja and bhāvana (contemplation) of Śrī Cakra form the corner-stones of Tāntric sādhana, the ordinary simple emotion of bhakti towards the Goddess has also its legitimate place in the system, as the Devī Bhāgavata amply testifies. (See especially Book VII, Chapter XXXVII) Accordingly, the *Lalitāsahasranāma* has such names as the following, indicative of this element:—

bhaktipriyā, bhaktigamyā, bhaktivaśyā, bhaktimat-kalpalatikā, bhakta-mānasa-hamsikā, bhakta-citta-kekighanā-ghanā, etc.

And, after all, it is these simple names inspired by genuine piety that possess universal validity, whereas the names that embody the doctrines of an arbitrary system or the details of a Purāṇic story can appeal only to the members of a sect. Hence the former constitute the most enduring and valuable part of the litany. The names dealing with the war against Bhaṇḍāsura and with the three-headed and four-headed Śaktis Rākiṇī and Lākinī that guard the cakras of the Kuṇḍalinī-Yoga, and even the names describing the physical beauty of the

Goddess, in spite of their sonorous language, are mere tinsel compared with the pure gold of the names that point to some aspect or other of the religious experience of men in all ages and countries. To this superior class belong such names as the following:

antarmukha - samārādhyā, bahirmukha - sudur - labhā, abhyāsātiśaya - jñātā, avyāja - karuṇā - mūrtiḥ, karūṇā - rasa - sāgarā, vandāru - jana - vatsalā, sadyaḥ - prasādinī, viśva - sākṣiṇī, sākṣi - varjitā, prema - rūpā, priyam - karī, svargāpavargadā, bhāva jnā, bhava - roga - ghnī, bhava - cakra - pravartinī, etc.

XV

It has to be admitted that there is a dark as well as a bright side to the Tāntric sādhana.

The fact seems to be that the worship of the Goddess, which, as we have seen, included many a tribal cult was in some parts of the country not fully assimilated to the orthodox Vedic religion. And so rituals and practices which that religion would have discouraged went on unchecked, and, when they invaded even the higher classes, they began to be justified by pseudo-philosophical theories based on some stray passages in the Vedic literature and were tolerated by others in accordance with the Hindu doctrine of adhikāra-bheda.

Hence arose two broad divisions among the worshippers of Śakti—those who followed the Vedic ritual and those who followed the non-Vedic Tāntric ritual. The former were supposed to belong to Dakṣiṇācāra and the latter to the Vāmācāra. Vāmācāra is defined in *Śabdakalpadruma* as vāmō viparīto, veda-viruddho vā, ācāraḥ.There are doctrinal as well as ritual differences between the two divisions of Śakti-worshippers:—

(1) The followers of Dakṣiṇācāra believe in the absolute equality of Śiva and Śakti; and they analyze this equality into equality of (i) adhiṣṭhāna (abode), (ii) anuṣṭhāna (occupation), (iii) avasthā (condition), (iv) rūpa (form) and nāma (name). Hence their faith is called Samaya mata. The *Śaundarya Laharī* (stanza 34) puts this equality in a nutshell. It says[2] that the relationship of seṣa and seṣī subsists *mutually* between Śiva and Śakti. During the creation and maintenance of the world the Śakti element predominates. But after pralaya, till creation starts again , the Śiva element predominates. On the other hand, the followers of Vāmācāra believe that Śakti is always predominant. For them Śiva is involved in Śakti. They do not recognize a separate Śiva-tattva. This

[1] It is best to translate these terms as 'traditional' and independent'.

[2] अतः शेषः शेषीत्ययमुभयसाधारणतया स्थितः संबन्धो वां

is represented symbolically by the figure of Śiva lying under the feet of Śakti.

(2) The Samayins believe that in the kuṇḍalinī-yoga sahasrārā is the goal, whereas the followers of Vāma believe that the kuṇḍalinī-śakti, after reaching sahasrāra and conferring bliss on the sādhaka, comes back to the mūlādhāra and sleeps there again. Hence, while the Samayins worship the Devī internally as stationed in sahasrāra, the Vāmas worship her externally in the two centres of mūlādhāra and svādhiṣṭhāna. Mūlādhāra is otherwise called Kula and the Devī occupying it is called Kaulinī and her worshippers are called Kaulas.

(3) For the Samayins the authoritative scriputures are the samhitas of Sanaka, Sananda, Sanatkumāra, Śuka and Vasiṣṭa, collectively known as Śubhāgama-pañcaka. For the Kaulas the authorities are Paraśurāma Sūtras and the sixty-four Tantras.

(4) The Ṛṣi of the Samayins is Dakṣiṇāmūrti, and their devatās are called Kāmeśvara and Kāmeśvarī. The Ṛṣi of the Kaulas is Bhairava, and their devatās are called Ānandabhairavī and Ānandabhairava.

(5) The external worship of the Samayins is according to the Kalpa-sutras of the Vedic tradition, and their offerings consist of milk and fruits. The worship of the Kaulas, on the other hand, is according to the

independent Tāntric ritēs involving offerings of what are known as Pañca-makāras.

The Samaya-mata is thus pure and noble. It is associated with the honoured name of Śaṅkara. The Kaulamata also is in many cases inoffensive, for, generally, harmless substitutes are introduced for the Pañca-makāras. Honey and ginger are used in the place of wine and a pumpkin or a coconut in the place of flesh—like *piṣṭa - paśu* in some of our yajnas. It is only with the extreme section of Kaulas—called Uttara Kaulas—that all those abominations which have brought Śāktism into disrepute are associated.

When there are two divisions in a sect, it is but natural that each should consider itself superior to the other. No wonder therefore that the Kaulas regard themselves as superior to and more advanced than the Samayins, as the Samayins regard Kaulamata as something belonging to the lower classes.

XVI

We are now in a position to understand the references in the *Lalitāsahasranāma* to the two main divisions among the Śāktas, *viz.*,the followers of Samayācāra and the followers of Kaulācāra. By calling Śiva and Śakti, Kāmeśvara and Kāmeśvarī in his litany and by giving the Goddess the names *samayā cāra* -

tatparā, samayāntasthā, sāma - rasya - parāyaṇā and *dakṣiṇāmūrti - svarūpiṇī,* the author aligns himself definitely on the side of the Dakṣiṇācāra. But he tries to hold the scales even by giving full recognition to the other school also. He indicates by various names that the worship by the Kaulas is equally acceptable to the Goddess. He calls her *kaula - mārgatatpara - sevitā, kula - sanketa - pālinī, kaulinī - kevalā, vīrā - rāḍhyā, vīra - goṣṭī - priyā,* etc., and probably refers to the secret rites of the Kaulas in the two names—*raho - yoga - kramārādhyā and rahastarpaṇa - tarpitā.* And he refers to the two ācāras together in the names *dakṣin'āḍakṣinārādhyā, savyāpasavya - margasthā,* and indicates that the Goddess could be reached by both the ways. But by calling the Goddess *durācāra-śamanī* and *duṣṭa-dūra* he condemns, of course, all evil ways and wicked men.

XVII

When we compare the *Lalitāsahasranāma* with the *Caṇḍī-māhātmya* we see what a great change has come over the worship of the Goddess through the influence of the Tāntric ideas. As in the earlier poem, we have in the *Lalitā* too references to the fight of the Goddess with a demon. But the war in the *Lalito-pākhyāna* is on a more refined plane, as Bhaṇḍa is a more refined Asura than the bison-headed Mahiṣa; and, as their names indicate, Lalitā represents the gentle side, and Caṇḍī the fierce side, of the Goddess. Probably both the fights were meant to be allegories. If so, Mahiṣa would be the beast in man and Bhaṇḍa the ego in man, and the Devī the divine spark in him. To realize the God in himself, man has to conquer first of all the beast in himself and, at a later stage, the egoism in himself. The second fight is on a much higher level and with superior weapons—Astras instead of Śastras. In the earlier fight, man resorts to laws and regulations, and in the later to prayer and contemplation. In truth, the battle on both the fronts is a never-ending one. For these Asuras never die. Slain in one form, they rise in another and renew the attack.

But, fortunately, it is the better side of the Tantras that has influenced the *Lalitāsahasranāma.* At the commencement of the poem the author describes at great length the person of the Goddess and refers throughout the litany to her marvellous beauty. Her jewels, her flowers, her smiles and glances and her likes and dislikes are all revealed to us with such exquisite skill that we feel the gracious presence of the Devī and believe that she is really, as the poet says, a *mahā-lāvaṇya-sevadhiḥ* —a treasure-house of beauty. From the point of view of pure poetry, this part of the *Sahasranāma* is the most artistic one. But we do not read the *Lalitā* for its poetry. We read it for its religious content. And from the point of view of religious thought, if we compare it with the odes in the *Caṇḍī-māhātmya* we are struck at once with its far wider range and its greater depth and variety. In the earlier work, as we have seen, it is the immanence of the deity that is stressed. In the *Lalitā* it is both the transcendence and the immanence that are stressed. In such names as *sat-asat-rūpa-dhāriṇī, satya-jñānānanda-rūpa, saccidānanda-rūpiṇī, nitya-śuddhā. nitya-buddhā niravadyā, nirantarā*—and there are about forty-five names beginning with such negatives—we see how deeply the litany is pervaded with Vedāntic thought. And we observe its strong Advaitic trend in such names as *nirdvaitā, dvaita-varjitā, brahmāt-maikya-svarūpiṇī, tattvamartha-svarūpiṇi, jñātṛ-jñeyạ-svarūpinī* and *mithyā-jagad-adhiṣṭhānā.* But what makes the *Lalitāsahasranāma* entirely different from the *Devī-māhātmya* and the earlier hymns to the Goddess is the predominant influence of Tāntric philosophy and sādhana. We have seen how the three great pillars of Tāntric teaching—the Pañcadaśī mantra, the Kuṇḍalinī yoga and the Śrī Cakra—stand out prominently in this noble and imposing structure of many halls and apartments which can give shelter to various classes of the devotees of the eternal Mother—Śrī-mātā, Śri-mahā-rājñī, Śrīmat-simhāsaneśvarī.

XVIII

As a literary form, the Sahasranāma is peculiar to Sanskrit literature, like the sūtra and the samāsa. Probably as a set-off against the prolixities and wild exaggerations of our popular literature, we have these elliptical, mnemonic literary forms from which every unnecessary word is removed. In the Sahasranāma the poet has to express his religious feelings and his philosophy of life, as well as his theological beliefs, through the names he coins for his deity. He has no room here for the elaboration of his subject, not even for logical connection between one statement and another. Topics have to be huddled together, like the words in a samāsa, without any connecting links. And, in a Sahasranāma, when samāsas themselves are huddled together without even a conjunction, the resulting structure is like a building in which the walls are formed by neatly chiselled stones being placed one above the other without any mortar or cement between them. Hence, as a literary form, the Sahasranāma has its own obvious disadvantages as well as advantages. If it encourages brevity and restraint, it also encourages incoherence and obscurity. When the poet is not required to show any logical connection he easily succumbs to the temptation of not conceiving any. The besetting drawback of many a Sahasranāma is that all logical thinking is sacrificed to the tin gods of alliteration and assonance. Hence we often have more sound than sense. Alliteration has, no doubt, a special value in such a mnemonic literary form as the Sahasranāma, but when it is secured at the expense of logical sequence it gives an uncomfortable jolt to the mind of the reader who is not content to be a mere parrot. In this respect the *Lalitāsahasranāma* is much better than many other Sahasranāmas. There is so much logical connection implied in the names that they easily fall into sections like those dealing with the physical form of the Goddess, her fight with Bhaṇḍāsura, her different abodes, her manifestations in the cakras of the human body and so on. But there are also many instances of want of logical sequence. For instance, the names (Nos. 844-846) *chandassāra, śāstrasāra, mantrasāra* are followed in the same line by *talodarī*—which means that the Goddess is the very essence of the Vedas, the essence of the Śāstras, the essence of Mantras and that she has a slender waist. Similarly, the very next line when translated literally would run as follows—'Her fame is extensive, her glory is boundless and she has the form of the letters of the alphabet'. Instances like these, which give a jolt to the intelligent reader and a headache to the conscientious translator, may be multiplied.

Again, the convention of having exactly one thousand names is more a disadvantage than an advantage. For, it is not always easy to devise a thousand names for the God or Goddess you worship without repeating yourself. And repetition of a name with the same meaning is forbidden by "the rules of the game". So, when the legitimate subject-matter is over in five or six hundred names the poet is forced to complete the list by something far-fetched or fanciful, just as in actual worship of the deity when all the flowers on hand are over we use coloured rice (akṣata) in their stead to complete the ritual. And if, by mischance, he repeats a name which has already been used, the commentator who comes in his wake has to rack his brains to give it a different meaning or cut it into two different bits and give some forced interpretation to each of the bits. Moreover, if logical connection has no leg to stand on even when coherent material is at hand, it vanishes into the thin air amidst these insubstantial word-juggleries. Fortunately, there are not many instances of these defects in the *Lalitāsahasranāma*. On the whole, the poet has been able to raise a very noble monument to the Goddess in spite of the exceedingly difficult literary form he has chosen to adopt here.

ध्यानम्

MEDITATION

सिन्दूरारुणविग्रहां त्रिनयनां माणिक्यमौलिस्फुरत्
तारानायकशेखरां स्मितमुखीमापीनवक्षोरुहाम् ।
पाणिभ्यामलिपूर्णरत्नचषकं रक्तोत्पलं बिभ्रतीं
सौम्यां रत्नघटस्थरक्तचरणां ध्यायेत्परामम्बिकाम् ॥

sindūrāruṇa-vigrahāṁ tri-nayanāṁ māṇikya
mauli-sphurat-
tārānāyaka-śekharāṁ smitamukhīm
āpīna-vakṣoruhām
pāṇibhyām alipūrṇa-ratna-caṣakaṁ
raktotpalaṁ bibhratīṁ
saumyāṁ ratna-ghaṭastha-rakta-caraṇāṁ
dhyāyetparāmambikām

The Divine Mother is to be meditated upon as shining in a vermilion-red body, with triple eyes, sporting a crown of rubies studded with the crescent moon, a face all smiles, a splendid bust, one hand holding a jewel-cup brimming with mead, and the other twirling a red lotus, beauty-personified having placed Her crimson feet on the pot made of precious stone.

अरुणां करुणातरङ्गिताक्षीं धृतपाशाङ्कुशपुष्पबाणचापाम् ।
अणिमादिभिरावृतां मयूखैरहमित्येव विभावये भवानीम् ॥

aruṇāṁ karuṇā-taraṅgitākṣīṁ
dhṛta-pāśāṅkuśa-puṣpa-bāṇa-cāpām
aṇimādibhir āvṛtām mayūkhai-
raham-ityeva vibhāvaye bhavānīm.

I think of Devi Bhavāni as the Supreme I-sense. She is rosy like the dawn, has eyes wherein surge waves of compassion and she holds in her four hands the noose, the goad, the flower-arrow and the sugar-cane bow. The effulgence of the eight siddhis beginning with minuteness surrounds her.

ध्यायेत् पद्मासनस्थां विकसितवदनां पद्मपत्रायताक्षीं
हेमाभां पीतवस्त्रां करकलितलसद्धेमपद्मां वराङ्गीम् ।
सर्वालङ्कारयुक्तां सततमभयदां भक्तनम्रां भवानीं
श्रीविद्यां शान्तमूर्तिं सकलसुरनुतां सर्वसम्पत्प्रदात्रीम् ॥

dhyāyet padmāsanasthām vikasita-vadanām
padma-patrāyatākṣīm
hemābhām pītavastrām kara-kalita-lasad-hema
padmām varāṅgīm
sarvālaṅkāra-yuktām satatam-abhayadām bhakta-
namrām bhavānīm

śrīvidyām śāntamūrtim sakala-sura-nutāṁ sarva sampat-pradātrīm.

Devi Bhavāni is ever to be contemplated upon as seated in a lotus, with a face beaming with joy, eyes soft and elongated like lotus petals, radiating a golden hue, dressed in yellow silk, sporting a golden lotus in her hand, perfect in every limb, profusely decorated, compassionate towards devotees, and bestowing protection and all prosperity on them. Adored by all celestials, she is the very embodiment of Śri Vidyā and Tranquillity.

सकुङ्कमविलेपनामलिकचुम्बिकस्तूरिकां
समन्दहसितेक्षणां सशरचापपाशांकुशाम्।
अशेषजनमोहिनीमरुणमाल्यभूषाम्बरां
जपाकुसुमभासुरां जपविधौ स्मरेदम्बिकाम् ॥

sakuṅkuma-vilepanām alika-cumbi-kastūrikām
samanda-hasitekṣaṇām saśara-cāpa-pāśāṅkuśām
aśeṣa-jana-mohinīm aruṇa-mālya-bhūṣāṁbarām
japā-kusuma-bhāsurām japavidhau smaredambikām

At the time of performing Japa we should meditate on the Mother, whose body is anointed all over with vermilion and musk that attracts the bees, whose glance itself is a lovely smile, who holds in her hands the bow, the arrow, the noose and the goad, who captivates every one without exception, who is adorned with red garlands and ornaments and who shines with the hue of the China rose.

॥ श्री ललिता-सहस्रनाम-स्तोत्रम् ॥

// *Srī Lalitā-sahasranāma-stotram* //

ओं श्रीमाता श्रीमहाराज्ञी श्रीमत्सिंहासनेश्वरी ।
चिदग्नि-कुण्ड-सम्भूता देवकार्य-समुद्यता ॥ 1 ॥

Śrīmātā śrī-mahārājñī śrīmat-simhāsan'eśvarī
cidagni-kuṇḍa-sambhūtā deva-kārya-samudyatā

उद्यद्भानु-सहस्राभा चतुर्बाहु-समन्विता ।
रागस्वरूप-पाशाढ्या क्रोधाकाराङ्कुशोज्ज्वला ॥ 2 ॥

Udyad-bhānu-sahasrābhā catur-bāhu-samanvitā
rāga-svarūpa-pāśā ḍhyā krodh'ākār'āṅkuś'ojjvalā

मनोरूपेक्षु-कोदण्डा पञ्चतन्मात्र-सायका ।
निजारुण-प्रभापूर-मज्जद्ब्रह्माण्ड-मण्डला ॥ 3 ॥

Mano-rūpekṣu-kodaṇḍā pañca-tanmātra-sāyakā
nijāruṇa-prabhāpūra-majjad-brahmāṇḍa-maṇḍalā

चम्पकाशोक-पुन्नाग-सौगन्धिक-लसत्कचा ।
कुरुविन्दमणि-श्रेणी-कनत्कोटीर-मण्डिता ॥ 4 ॥

Campak'āśoka-punnāga-saugandhika-lasat-kacā
kuruvinda-maṇi-śreṇī-kanat-kotīra-maṇḍitā

अष्टमीचन्द्र-विभ्राज-दलिकस्थल-शोभिता ।
मुखचन्द्र-कलङ्काभ-मृगनाभि-विशेषका ॥ 5 ॥

Aṣṭamī-candra-vibhrāja-dalika-sthala-śobhitā
mukha-candra-kalaṇkābha mṛga-nābhi-viśeṣakā

वदनस्मर-माङ्गल्य-गृहतोरण-चिल्लिका ।
वक्त्रलक्ष्मी-परीवाह-चलन्मीनाभ-लोचना ॥ 6 ॥

Vadana-smara-māṅgalya-gṛha-toraṇa-cillikā
vaktra-lakṣmī-parīvāha-calan-mīnābha-locanā

नवचम्पक-पुष्पाभ-नासादण्ड-विराजिता ।
ताराकान्ति-तिरस्कारि-नासाभरण-भासुरा ॥ 7 ॥

Nava-campaka-puṣpābha-nāsā-daṇḍa-virājitā
tārā-kānti-tiraskāri-nāsābharaṇa-bhāsurā

कदम्बमञ्जरी-क्लृप्त-कर्णपूर-मनोहरा ।
ताटङ्क-युगली-भूत-तपनोडुप-मण्डला ॥ 8 ॥

Kadamba-mañjarī-klpta-karṇa-pūra-manoharā
tāṭaṅka-yugalībhūta-tapanoḍupa-maṇḍalā

पद्मरागशिलादर्श-परिभावि-कपोलभूः ।
नवविद्रुम-बिम्बश्री-न्यक्कारि-रदनच्छदा ॥ 9 ॥

Padma-rāga-śilādarśa-paribhāvi-kapolabhūḥ
nava-vidruma-bimba-śrī-nyakkāri- raśana - cchadā

शुद्धविद्यांकुराकार-द्विजपंक्ति-द्वयोज्ज्वला ।
कर्पूरवीटिकामोद-समाकर्षि-दिगन्तरा ॥ 10 ॥

Śuddha-vidy'āṅkur'ākāra-dvija-paṅkti-dvay'ojj-vala
karpūra-vīṭikāmoda-samākarṣi-digantarā

निज-संलाप-माधुर्य-विनिर्भर्त्सित-कच्छपी ।
मन्दस्मित-प्रभापूर-मज्जत्कामेश-मानसा ॥ 11 ॥
Nija-sallāpa-mādhurya-vinirbhartsita-kacchapī
manda-smita-prabhā-pūra-majjat-kāmeśa-mānasā

अनाकलित-सादृश्य-चिबुकश्री-विराजिता ।
कामेश-बद्ध-मांगल्य-सूत्र-शोभित-कन्धरा ॥ 12 ॥
Anākalita-sādṛśya-cibuka-śrī-virājitā
kāmeśa-baddha-māṅgalya-sūtra-śobhita-kandharā

कनकांगद-केयूर-कमनीय-भुजान्विता ।
रत्नग्रैवेय-चिन्ताक-लोल-मुक्ता-फलान्विता ॥ 13 ॥
Kanak'āṅgada-keyūra-kamanīya-bhujānvitā
ratna-graiveya-cintāka-lola-muktā-phalānvitā

कामेश्वर-प्रेमरत्न-मणि-प्रतिपण-स्तनी ।
नाभ्यालवाल-रोमालि-लता-फल-कुचद्वयी ॥ 14 ॥

Kāmeśvara-prema-ratna-maṇi-pratipaṇa-stanī
nābhyāla-vāla-romāli-latāphala-kuca-dvayī

लक्ष्यरोम-लताधारता-समुन्नेय-मध्यमा ।
स्तनभार-दलन्मध्य-पट्टबन्ध-वलित्रया ॥ 15 ॥

Lakṣya-roma-latā-dhāratā-samunneya-madhyamā
stana-bhāra-dalan-madhya-paṭṭa-bandha
-vali-trayā

अरुणारुणकौसुंभ-वस्त्र-भास्वत्-कटीतटी ।
रत्न-किंकिणिका-रम्य-रशना-दाम-भूषिता ॥ 16 ॥

Aruṇāruṇa-kausumbha-vastra-bhāsvat-kaṭī-taṭī
ratna-kiṅkiṇikā-ramya-raśanā-dāma-bhūṣitā

कामेश-ज्ञात-सौभाग्य-मार्दवोरु-द्वयान्विता
माणिक्य-मुकुटाकार-जानुद्वय-विराजिता ॥ 17 ॥

Kāmeśa-jñāta-saubhāgya-mārda'voru-dvayānvitā
māṇikya-mukuṭ'ākara-jānudvaya-virājitā

इन्द्रगोप-परिक्षिप्तस्मरतूणाभ-जंघिका ।
गूढगुल्फा कूर्मपृष्ठ-जयिष्णु-प्रपदान्विता ॥ 18 ॥

Indra-gopa-parikṣipta-smara-tūṇābha-jaṅghikā
gūḍha-gulphā kūrma-pṛṣṭha-jayiṣṇu-prapadānvitā

नख दीधिति-संछन्न-नमज्जन-तमोगुणा ।
पदद्वय-प्रभाजाल-पराकृत-सरोरुहा ॥ 19 ॥

Nakha-dīdhiti-saṁchanna-namajjana-tamoguṇā
pada-dvaya-prabhājāla-parākṛta-saroruhā

सिंजान-मणिमंजीर मण्डित-श्री-पदांबुजा ।
मराली-मन्दगमना महालावण्य-शेवधिः ॥ 20 ॥

Siñjāna-maṇi-manjīra-maṇḍita-śrī-padāmbujā
marālī-manda-gamanā-mahālāvaṇya-śevadhiḥ

सर्वारुणाऽनवद्यांगी सर्वाभरण-भूषिता ।
शिव-कामेश्वरांकस्था शिवा स्वाधीन-वल्लभा ॥ 21 ॥

Sarv'āruṇ'ā navadyāṅgī sarv'ābharaṇa-bhūṣitā
śiva-kāmeśvar'āṅkasthā śivā svādhīna-vallabhā

सुमेरु-मध्य-श्रृंगस्था श्रीमन्नगर-नायिका ।
चिन्तामणि गृहान्तस्था पंच-ब्रह्मासन-स्थिता ॥ 22 ॥

Sumeru-madhya-śṛṅgasthā-śriman-nagara-nāyikā
cintāmaṇi-gṛh'āntasthā pañca-brahm'āsana-sthitā

महापद्माटवी-संस्था कदंबवन-वासिनी
सुधासागर-मध्यस्था कामाक्षी कामदायिनी ॥ 23 ॥

Mahā-padmāṭavī-samsthā kadamba-vana-vāsinī
sudhā-sāgara-madhyasthā kāmāksī kāmadāyinī

देवर्षि-गण-संघात-स्तूयमानात्म-वैभवा ।
भण्डासुर-वधोद्युक्त-शक्तिसेना-समन्विता ॥ 24 ॥

Devarṣi-gaṇa-saṅghāta-stūyamān'ātma-vaibhavā
bhaṇḍāsura-vadh'odyukta-śakti-senā-samanvitā

संपत्करी-समारूढ-सिंधुर-व्रज-सेविता ।
अश्वारूढाधिष्ठिताश्व-कोटि-कोटिभि-रावृता ॥ 25 ॥

Sampatkarī-samārūḍha-sindhura-vraja-sevitā
aśvārūḍh'ā´dhiṣṭit'āśva-koṭi-koṭibhir-āvṛtā

चक्रराज-रथारूढ-सर्वायुध-परिष्कृता ।
गेयचक्र-रथारूढ-मंत्रिणी-परिसेविता ॥ 26 ॥

Cakrarāja-rathārūḍha-sarvāyudha-pariṣkṛtā
geya-cakra-rath'ārūḍha-mantriṇī-parisevitā

किरिचक्र-रथारूढ-दण्डनाथा-पुरस्कृता ।
ज्वालामालिनिकाक्षिप्त-वह्निप्राकार-मध्यगा ॥ 27 ॥

Kiricakra-rathārūḍha-daṇḍanāthā-puraskṛtā
jvālā-mālinik'ākṣipta-vahni-prākāra-madhyagā

भण्डसैन्य-वधोद्युक्त-शक्ति-विक्रम-हर्षिता ।
नित्या-पराक्रमाटोप-निरीक्षण-समुत्सुका ॥ 28 ॥

Bhaṇḍa-sainya-vadh'odyukta-śakti-vik-
rama-harsitā
nityā-parākram'āṭopa-nirīkṣaṇa-samutsukā

भण्डपुत्र-वधोद्युक्त-बाला-विक्रम-नन्दिता ।
मन्त्रिण्यंबा-विरचित-विषंग-वध-तोषिता ॥ 29 ॥

Bhaṇḍaputra-vadh'odyukta-bālā-vikrama-nanditā
mantriṇyambā-viracita-viṣaṅga-vadha-toṣitā

विशुक्र-प्राणहरण-वाराही-वीर्य-नंदिता ।
कामेश्वर-मुखालोक-कल्पित-श्रीगणेश्वरा ॥ 30 ॥

Viśukra-prāṇa-haraṇa-vārāhī-vīrya-nanditā
kāmeśvara-mukhāloka-kalpita-śrīgaṇeśvarā

महागणेश-निर्भिन्न-विघ्नयन्त्र-प्रहर्षिता ।
भण्डासुरेन्द्र-निर्मुक्त-शस्त्र-प्रत्यस्त्र-वर्षिणी ॥ 31 ॥

Mahā-gaṇeśa- nirbhinna-vighna-yantra-praharṣitā
Bhaṇḍ-āsurendra-nir-
mukta-śastra-pratyastra-varṣiṇī

करांगुलि-नखोत्पन्न-नारायण-दशाकृतिः ।
महा-पाशुपतास्त्राग्नि-निर्दग्धासुर-सैनिका ॥ 32 ॥

Karāṅguli-nakh-otpanna-nārāyaṇa-daśākṛtiḥ
mahā-pāśupat'āstrāgni-nirdagdh āsura-sainikā

कामेश्वरास्त्र-निर्दग्ध-सभण्डासुर-शून्यका ।
ब्रह्मोपेन्द्र-महेन्द्रादि-देव-संस्तुत-वैभवा ॥ 33 ॥

Kāmeṣvar'āśtra-nirdagdha-sabhaṇḍ'āsura-śūnyakā

brahm'opendra-mahendr'ādi-deva-samstuta-
vaibhavā

हर-नेत्राग्नि-संदग्ध-काम-संजीवनौषधिः ।
श्रीमद्वाग्भव-कूटैक-स्वरूप-मुख-पंकजा ॥ 34 ॥

Haranetrāgni-samdagdha-kāma-sañjīvan'auṣadhiḥ
śrīmad-vāgbhava-kūṭaika-svarūpa-mukha-paṅkajā

कण्ठाधः-कटि-पर्यन्त-मध्यकूट-स्वरूपिणी ।
शक्तिकूटैकतापन्न-कठ्यधोभाग -धारिणी ॥ 35 ॥

Kaṇṭhādhaḥ-kaṭi-paryanta-madhya-kūṭa
-svarūpiṇī
śakti-kūṭ'aikat'āpanna- kaṭhy'adhobhāga-dhāriṇī

मूलमन्त्रात्मिका मूलकूटत्रय-कलेबरा ।
कुलामृतैक-रसिका कुलसंकेत-पालिनी ॥ 36 ॥

Mūla-mantr'ātmikā-mūla-kūṭa-traya-kalebarā
kul'āmṛtaika-rasikā kula-samketa-pālinī

कुलांगना कुलान्तस्था कौलिनी कुलयोगिनी ।
अकुला समयान्तस्था समयाचार-तत्परा ॥ 37 ॥

Kulāṅganā kul'āntasthā kaulinī kulayoginī
akulā samay'āntasthā samay'ācāra-tatparā

मूलाधारैक-निलया ब्रह्मग्रन्थि-विभेदिनी ।
मणिपूरान्तरुदिता विष्णुग्रन्थि-विभेदिनी ॥ 38 ॥
Mūlādhāraika-nilayā brahma-granthi-vibhedinī
maṇi-pūr'āntaruditā viṣṇu-granthi-vibhedinī

आज्ञाचक्रान्तरालस्था रुद्रग्रन्थि-विभेदिनी ।
सहस्रारांबुजारूढा सुधासाराभिवर्षिणी ॥ 39 ॥
Ājñā-cakr'āntarālasthā rudra-granthi-vibhedinī
sahasrār'āmbuj'āruḍhā sudhā sārābhi-varṣiṇı

तडिल्लता समरुचिः षट्चक्रोपरि-संस्थिता ।
महासक्तिः कुण्डलिनी बिसतन्तु-तनीयसी ॥ 40 ॥

Taḍil-latā samarucih ṣaṭ-cakr'opari-samsthitā
mahā-saktiḥ kuṇḍalinī bisatantu-tanīyasī

भवानी भावनागम्या भवारण्य-कुठारिका ।
भद्रप्रिया भद्रमूर्ति-र्भक्त-सौभाग्यदायिनी ॥ 41 ॥

Bhavānī bhāvanāgamyā bhavāraṇya-kuthārikā
bhadra-priyā bhadra-mūrtir-bhakta-saubhāgya
-dāyini

भक्तिप्रिया भक्तिगम्या भक्तिवश्या भयापहा ।
शांभवी शारदाराध्या शर्वाणी शर्मदायिनी ॥ 42 ॥

Bhakti-priyā Bhaktı-gamyā bhakti-vaśyā
bhay-āpahā
śāmbhavī śārad'ārādhyā śarvāṇī śarma-dāyinī

शांकरी श्रीकरी साध्वी शरच्चन्द्र-निभानना ।
शातोदरी शान्तिमती निराधारा निरंजना ॥ 43 ॥

Śāmkarī śrīkarī sādhvī śarac-candra-nibhānanā
śātodarī śāntimatī nirādhārā nirañjanā

निर्लेपा निर्मला नित्या निराकारा निराकुला ।
निर्गुणा निष्कला शान्ता निष्कामा निरुपप्लवा ॥ 44 ॥

Nirlepā nirmalā nityā nirākārā nirākulā
nirguṇā niṣkalā śāntā niṣkāmā nirupaplavā

नित्यमुक्ता निर्विकारा निष्प्रपंचा निराश्रया ।
नित्यशुद्धा नित्यबुद्धा निरवद्या निरन्तरा ॥ 45 ॥

Nitya-muktā nirvikārā niṣprapañcā nirāśrayā
nitya-śuddhā nitya-buddhā niravadyā nirantarā

निष्कारणा निष्कलंका निरुपाधि-र्निरीश्वरा ।
नीरागा रागमथनी निर्मदा मदनाशिनी ॥ 46 ॥

Niṣkāraṇā niṣkalamkā nirupādhir-nirīśvarā
nīrāgā rāga-mathanī nirmadā mada-nāśinī

निश्चिन्ता निरहंकारा निर्मोहा मोहनाशिनी ।
निर्ममा ममताहन्त्री निष्पापा पापनाशिनी ॥ 47 ॥

Niścintā nirahamkārā nirmohā moha-nāśinī
nirmamā mamatā-hantrī niṣpāpā pāpa-nāśinī

निष्क्रोधा क्रोधशमनी निर्लोभा लोभनाशिनी ।
निःसंशया संशयघ्नी निर्भवा भवनाशिनी ॥ 48 ॥

Niṣkrodhā krodha-śamanī nirlobhā lobha-nāśinī
niḥ-samśayā samśaya-ghnī nirbhavā bhava-nāśinī

निर्विकल्पा निराबाधा निर्भेदा भेदनाशिनी ।
निर्नाशा मृत्युमथनी निष्क्रिया निष्परिग्रहा ॥ 49 ॥

Nirvikalpā nirābādhā nirbhedā bheda-nāśinī
nirnāśā mṛtyu-mathanī niṣkriyā niṣparigrahā

निस्तुला नीलचिकुरा निरपाया निरत्यया ।
दुर्लभा दुर्गमा दुर्गा दुःखहन्त्री सुखप्रदा ॥ 50 ॥

Nistulā nīla-cikurā nırapāyā niratyayā
durlabhā durgamā durgā duḥkha-hantrī
sukha-pradā

दुष्टदूरा दुराचारशमनी दोष-वर्जिता ।
सर्वज्ञा सान्द्रकरुणा समानाधिक-वर्जिता ॥ 51 ॥

Duṣṭadūrā durācāra-śamanī doṣā-varjitā
sarvajñā sāndrakaruṇā samānādhika-varjitā

सर्वशक्तिमयी सर्वमंगला सद्गति-प्रदा ।
सर्वेश्वरी सर्वमयी सर्वमन्त्र-स्वरूपिणी ॥ 52 ॥

Sarva-śaktimayī sarva-maṅgalā sad-gati-pradā
sarv'eśvarī sarvamayī sarva-mantra-svarūpiṇī

सर्व-यन्त्रात्मिका सर्व-तन्त्ररूपा मनोन्मनी ।
माहेश्वरी महादेवी महालक्ष्मी-मृडप्रिया ॥ 53 ॥

Sarva-yantr'ātmikā sarva-tantra-rūpā manonmanī
māheśvarī mahādevī mahālakṣmī mṛḍapriyā

महारूपा महापूज्या महा-पातक-नाशिनी ।
महामाया महासत्वा महाशक्ति-र्महारतिः ॥ 54 ॥

Mahārūpā mahāpūjyā mahā-pātaka-nāśinī
mahāmāyā mahāsattvā mahā-śaktir mahā-ratiḥ

महाभोगा महैश्वर्या महावीर्या महाबला ।
महाबुद्धि-र्महासिद्धि-र्महायोगेश्वरेश्वरी ॥ 55 ॥

Mahābhogā mah'aiśvaryā mahāvīryā mahābalā
mahābuddhir mahāsiddhir mahāyog'eśvar'eśvarī

महातन्त्रा महामन्त्रा महायन्त्रा महासना ।
महायाग-क्रमाराध्या महाभैरव-पूजिता ॥ 56 ॥

Mahātantrā mahāmantrā mahāyantrā mahāsanā
mahāyāga-kram'ārādhyā mahā bhairava-pūjitā

महेश्वर-महाकल्प-महाताण्डव-साक्षिणी ।
महाकामेश-महिषी महात्रिपुरसुन्दरी ॥ 57 ॥

Maheśvara-mahākalpa-mahātāṇḍava-sākṣiṇī
mahākāmeśa-mahiṣī mahātripura sundarī

चतुष्षष्ट्युपचाराढ्या चतुष्षष्टिकलामयी ।
महाचतुः-षष्टिकोटि-योगिनी-गणसेविता ॥ 58 ॥

Catuṣ-ṣaṣṭyupacārāḍhyā catuṣ-ṣaṣṭi-kalāmayī
mahācatuḥ-ṣaṣṭikoṭi-yoginī-gaṇasevıta

मनुविद्या चन्द्रविद्या चन्द्रमण्डल-मध्यगा ।
चारुरूपा चारुहासा चारुचन्द्र-कलाधरा ॥ 59 ॥

Manuvidyā candravidyā candramaṇḍala-
madhyagā
cārurūpā cāruhāsā cārucandra-kalādharā

चराचर-जगन्नाथा चक्रराज-निकेतना ।
पार्वती पद्मनयना पद्मराग-समप्रभा ॥ 60 ॥

Carācara-jagannāthā cakrarāja-niketanā
pārvatī padmanayanā padmarāga-samaprabhā

पंचप्रेतासनासीना पंचब्रह्मस्वरूपिणी ।
चिन्मयी परमानन्दा विज्ञानघनरूपिणी ॥ 61 ॥

Pañcapretāsanāsīnā pañca-brahma-svarūpiṇī
cinmayī paramānandā vijñāna-ghana-rūpiṇī

ध्यान-ध्यातृ-ध्येयरूपा धर्माधर्म-विवर्जिता ।
विश्वरूपा जागरिणी स्वपन्ती तैजसात्मिका ॥ 62 ॥

Dhyāna-dhyātṛ-dhyeyarūpā dharmādharma vivarjitā
viśva-rūpā jāgariṇī svapantī taijasātmikā

सुप्ता प्राज्ञात्मिका तुर्या सर्वावस्था-विवर्जिता ।
सृष्टिकर्त्री ब्रह्मरूपा गोप्त्री गोविन्दरूपिणी ॥ 63 ॥

Suptā prājñātmikā turyā sarvāvasthā-vivarjitā
sṛṣṭikartrī brahmarūpā goptrī govindarūpiṇī

संहारिणी रुद्ररूपा तिरोधानकरीश्वरी ।
सदाशिवाऽनुग्रहदा पंचकृत्यपरायणा ॥ 64 ॥

Saṃhāriṇī rudrarūpā tirodhānakarīśvarī
sadāśivā' nugrahadā pañca-kṛtyaparāyaṇā

भानुमण्डल-मध्यस्था भैरवी भगमालिनी ।
पद्मासना भगवती पद्मनाभ-सहोदरी ॥ 65 ॥

Bhānumaṇḍala-madhyasthā bhairavī bhagamālinī
padm'āsanā bhagavatī padma-nābha-sahodarī

उन्मेष-निमिषोत्पन्न-विपन्न-भुवनावली ।
सहस्रशीर्षवदना सहस्राक्षी सहस्रपात् ॥ 66 ॥

Unmeṣa-nimiṣ'otpanna-vipanna-bhuvanāvalī
sahasra-śīrṣa-vadanā sahasrākṣī sahasrapāt

आब्रह्म -कीट-जननी वर्णाश्रम-विधायिनी ।
निजाज्ञारूप-निगमा पुण्यापुण्य-फलप्रदा ॥ 67 ॥

Ābrahma-kīṭa-jananī varṇāśrama-vidhāyinī
nij'ājñā-rūpa-nigamā puṇy' āpuṇya-phala-pradā

श्रुति-सीमन्त-सिन्दूरी-कृत-पादाब्जधूलिका ।
सकलागम-संदोह-शुक्ति-संपुट-मौक्तिका ॥ 68 ॥

Śruti-sīmanta-sindūrī-kṛta-pādābja-dhūlikā
sakal'āgama-sandoha-śukti-sampuṭa-mauktikā

पुरुषार्थ-प्रदा पूर्णा भोगिनी भुवनेश्वरी ।
अंबिकाऽनादि-निधना हरिब्रह्मेन्द्र-सेविता ॥ 69 ॥

Puruṣārtha-pradā pūrṇā bhoginī bhuvaneśvarī
ambik'ānādi-nidhanā hari-brahm'endra-sevitā

नारायणी नादरूपा नामरूप-विवर्जिता ।
ह्रींकारीह्रीमती हृद्या हेयोपादेय-वर्जिता ॥ 70 ॥

Nārāyaṇī nādarūpā nāmarūpa-vivarjitā
hrīnkārī hrīmatī hṛdyā hey'opādeya-varjitā

राजराजार्चिता राज्ञी रम्या राजीव-लोचना ।
रंजनी रमणी रस्या रणत्किंकिणि-मेखला ॥ 71 ॥

Rāja-rāj'ārcitā rājñī ramyā rājīva-locanā
rañjanī ramaṇī rasyā raṇat-kiṅkiṇi-mekhalā

रमा राकेन्दु-वदना रतिरूपा रतिप्रिया ।
रक्षाकरी राक्षसघ्नी रामा रमणलंपटा ॥ 72 ॥

Ramā rākendu-vadanā ratirūpā ratipriyā
rakṣākarī rākṣasaghnī rāmā ramaṇa-lampaṭā

काम्या कामकलारूपा कदंब-कुसुम-प्रिया ।
कल्याणी जगती-कन्दा करुणा-रस-सागरा ॥ 73 ॥

Kāmyā kāmakalārūpā kadamba-kusuma-priyā
kalyāṇī jagatī-kandā karuṇā-rasa-sāgarā

कलावती कलालापा कान्ता कादंबरी-प्रिया ।
वरदा वामनयना वारुणी-मद-विह्वला ॥ 74 ॥

Kalāvatī kalālāpā kāntā kādambarī-priyā
varadā vāmanayanā vāruṇī-mada-vihvalā

विश्वाधिका वेदवेद्या विन्ध्याचल-निवासिनी ।
विधात्री वेदजननी विष्णुमाया विलासिनी ॥ 75 ॥

Viśvādhikā vedavedyā vindhy'ācala-nivāsinī
vidhātrī vedajananī viṣṇumāyā vilāsinī

क्षेत्रस्वरूपा क्षेत्रेशी क्षेत्र-क्षेत्रज्ञ-पालिनी ।
क्षयवृद्धि-विनिर्मुक्ता क्षेत्रपाल-समर्चिता ॥ 76 ॥

Kṣetrasvarūpā kṣetreśī kṣetra-kṣetrajña-pālinī
kṣayavṛddhi-vinirmuktā Kṣetrapāla-samarcitā

विजया विमला वन्द्या वन्दारु-जन-वत्सला ।
वाग्वादिनी वामकेशी वह्निमण्डल-वासिनी ॥ 77 ॥

Vijayā vimalā vandyā vandāru-jana-vatsalā
vāgvādinī vāmakeśī vahni-maṇḍala-vāsinī

भक्तिमत्-कल्पलतिका पशुपाश-विमोचिनी ।
संहृताशेष-पाषण्डा सदाचार-प्रवर्तिका ॥ 78 ॥

Bhaktimat-kalpalatikā paśu-pāśa-vimocinī
samhṛt'āśeṣa pāṣaṇḍā sadācāra-pravartikā

तापत्रयाग्नि-संतप्त-समाह्लादन-चन्द्रिका ।
तरुणी तापसाराध्या तनुमध्या तमोपहा ॥ 79 ॥

Tāpa-tray'āgni-samtapta-sam'āhlādana-candrikā
taruṇī tāpas'ārādhyā tanu-madhyā tamopahā

चिति-स्तत्पद-लक्ष्यार्था चिदेकरस-रूपिणी ।
स्वात्मानन्द-लवीभूत-ब्रह्माद्यानन्द-सन्ततिः ॥ 80 ॥

Citis tatpada-lakṣyā'arthā-cid'ekarasa-rūpiṇī
svātm'ānanda-lavībhūta-brahm'ādy'ānanda-
santatiḥ

परा प्रत्यक्-चितीरूपा पश्यन्ती परदेवता ।
मध्यमा वैखरी-रूपा भक्त-मानस-हंसिका ॥ 81 ॥

Parā pratyak-citīrūpā paśyantī para-devatā
madhyamā vaikharī-rūpā bhakta-mānasa-hamsikā

कामेश्वर-प्राणनाडी कृतज्ञा कामपूजिता ।
शृंगार-रस-संपूर्णा जया जालंधर-स्थिता ॥ 82 ॥

Kāmeśvara-prāṇanāḍī kṛtajñā kāmapūjitā
śṛṅgāra-rasa-sampūrṇā jayā jālandharasthitā

ओड्याण-पीठ-निलया बिन्दु-मण्डलवासिनी ।
रहोयाग-क्रमाराध्या रहस्तर्पण-तर्पिता ॥ 83 ॥

Oḍyāṇa-pīṭha-nilayā bindu-maṇḍala-vāsinī
raho-yāga-kram'ārādhyā rahas-tarpaṇa-tarpitā

सद्यःप्रसादिनी विश्वसाक्षिणी साक्षिवर्जिता ।
षडंगदेवता-युक्ता षाड्गुण्य-परिपूरिता ॥ 84 ॥

Sadyaḥ-prasādinī viśva-sākṣiṇī sākṣi-varjitā
Ṣaḍ-aṅga-devatā-yuktā ṣāḍ-guṇya-paripūritā

नित्य-क्लिन्ना निरुपमा निर्वाण-सुख-दायिनी ।
नित्याषोडशिका-रूपा श्रीकण्ठार्ध-शरीरिणी ॥ 85 ॥

Nitya-klinnā nırupamā nirvāṇa-sukha-dāyinī
nityā-ṣoḍaśikā-rūpā śrīkaṇṭhardha-śarīriṇī

प्रभावती प्रभारूपा प्रसिद्धा परमेश्वरी ।
मूलप्रकृति-रव्यक्ता व्यक्ताव्यक्त-स्वरूपिणी ॥ 86 ॥

Prabhāvatī prabhārūpā prasiddhā param'eśvarī
mūla-prakṛtir avyaktā vyakt'ā vyakta-svarūpiṇī

व्यापिनी विविधाकारा विद्याविद्या-स्वरूपिणी ।
महाकामेश-नयन-कुमुदाह्लाद-कौमुदी ॥ 87 ॥

Vyāpinī vivdh'ākārā vidy'āvidyā-svarūpiṇī
mahā-kāmeśa-nayana-kumud'āhlāda-kaumudī

भक्त-हार्द-तमो-भेद-भानुमद्भानु-सन्ततिः ।
शिवदूती शिवाराध्या शिवमूर्तिः शिवंकरी ॥ 88 ॥

Bhakta-hārda-tamo-bheda-bhānumat-bhānu-
santatiḥ
śiva-dūtī śivārādhyā śivamūrtiḥ śivam-karī

शिवप्रिया शिवपरा शिष्टेष्टा शिष्टपूजिता ।
अप्रमेया स्वप्रकाशा मनो-वाचामगोचरा ॥ 89 ॥

Śivapriyā śivaparā śiṣṭeṣṭā śiṣṭapūjitā
aprameyā sva-prakāśā mano-vācām-agocarā

चिच्छक्ति-श्चेतना-रूपा जडशक्ति-र्जडात्मिका ।
गायत्री व्याहृतिः संध्या द्विजबृन्द-निषेविता ।। 90 ।।

Cicchaktiś cetanā-rūpā jaḍaśaktir jaḍātmikā
gāyatrī vyāhṛtiḥ sandhyā dvijabṛnda-niṣevitā

तत्वासना तत्वमयी पंचकोशान्तर-स्थिता ।
निःसीम-महिमा नित्य-यौवना मदशालिनी ।। 91 ।।

Tatv'āsanā tatvamayī pañca-koś'āntara-sthitā
niḥsīma-mahimā nitya-yauvanā mada-śālinī

मदघूर्णित-रक्ताक्षी मदपाटल-गण्डभूः ।
चन्दन-द्रव-दिग्धांगी चांपेय-कुसुम-प्रिया ।। 92 ।।

Mada-ghūrṇita-raktākṣī mada-pāṭala-gaṇḍa-bhūḥ
candana-drava-digdhāṅgī cāmpeya-kusuma-priyā

कुशला कोमलाकारा कुरुकुल्ला कुलेश्वरी ।
कुलकुण्डालया कौलमार्ग-तत्पर-सेविता ।। 93 ।।

Kuśalā komal'ākārā kurukullā kuleśvarī
kula-kuṇḍ'ālayā kaula-mārga-tatpara-sevitā

कुमार-गणनाथांबा तुष्टिः पुष्टि-र्मति-र्धृतिः ।
शान्तिः स्वस्तिमती कान्ति-र्नन्दिनी विघ्ननाशिनी ।। 94 ।।

Kumāra-gaṇa-nāth'āmbā tuṣṭiḥ puṣṭir
matir dhṛtiḥ
śāntiḥ svastimatī kāntir nandinī vighna-nāśinī

तेजोवती त्रिनयना लोलाक्षी-कामरूपिणी ।
मालिनी हंसिनी माता मलयाचल-वासिनी ॥ 95 ॥

Tejovatī trinayanā lolākṣī - kāmarūpiṇī
mālinī hamsinī mātā malayācala - vāsinī

सुमुखी नलिनी सुभ्रूः शोभना सुरनायिका ।
कालकण्ठी कान्तिमती क्षोभिणी सूक्ष्मरूपिणी ॥ 96 ॥

Sumukhī nalinī subhrūḥ śobhanā suranāyikā
kālakaṇṭhī kāntimatī kṣobhiṇī sūkṣma-rūpiṇī

वज्रेश्वरी वामदेवी वयोवस्था-विवर्जिता ।
सिद्धेश्वरी सिद्धविद्या सिद्धमाता यशस्विनी ॥ 97 ॥

Vajr'eśvarī vāmadevī vay'ovasthā - vivarjitā
siddh'eśvarī siddha-vidyā siddha-mātā yaśasvinī

विशुद्धिचक्र-निलया-ऽऽरक्तवर्णा त्रिलोचना ।
खट्वांगादि-प्रहरणा वदनैक-समन्विता ॥ 98 ॥

Viśuddhi-cakra-nilay'āraktavarṇā tri'locanā
khaṭvāṅgādi -praharaṇa vadan'aika - samanvitā

पायसान्न-प्रिया त्वक्स्था पशुलोक-भयंकरी ।
अमृतादि-महाशक्ति-संवृता डाकिनीश्वरी ॥ 99 ॥

Pāyasānna-priyā tvaksthā paśuloka - bhayamkarī
amṛtādi - mahāśakti - samvṛtā ḍākin'īśvarī

अनाहताब्ज-निलया श्यामाभा वदनद्वया ।
दंष्ट्रोज्ज्वलाक्षमालादि-धरा रुधिर-संस्थिता ॥ 100 ॥

Anāhatābja-nilayā śyāmabhā vadanadvayā
damṣṭr'ojjval'ākṣa-mālādi-dharā rudhira-samsthitā

कालरात्र्यादि-शक्त्यौघ-वृता स्निग्धौदन-प्रिया ।
महावीरेन्द्र-वरदा राकिण्यंबा-स्वरूपिणी ॥ 101 ॥

Kāla-rātryādi -śakty 'augha-vṛtā snigdh'audana-priyā
mahā-vīrendra-varadā rākiṇy-ambā svarūpinī

मणिपूराब्ज-निलया वदनत्रय-संयुता ।
वज्रादिकायुधोपेता डामर्यादिभि-रावृता ॥ 102 ॥

Maṇipūr'ābja-nilayā vadanatraya-samyutā
vajrādik'āyudhopetā ḍāmaryādibhir-āvṛtā

रक्तवर्णा मांसनिष्ठा गुडान्न-प्रीत-मानसा ।
समस्तभक्त-सुखदा लाकिन्यंबा-स्वरूपिणी ॥ 103 ॥

Rakta-varṇā māmsa-niṣṭhā guḍānna-prīta-mānasā
samasta-bhakta-sukhadā lākiny'ambā-svarūpiṇī

स्वाधिष्ठानांबुजगता चतुर्वक्त्र-मनोहरा ।
शूलाद्यायुध-संपन्ना पीतवर्णातिगर्विता ॥ 104 ॥

Svādhiṣṭhān' āmbuja-gatā catur-vaktra-manoharā
śūl'ādy'āyudha - sampannā pītavarṇ'ātigarvitā

मेदो-निष्ठा मधुप्रीता बन्धिन्यादि-समन्विता ।
दध्यन्नासक्त-हृदया काकिनी-रूप-धारिणी ॥ 105 ॥

Medo-niṣṭhā madhu-prītā bandhiny'ādi-samanvitā
dadhy'an n'āsakta-hṛdayā kākinī-rūpa-dhāriṇī

मूलाधारांबुजारूढा पंचवक्त्रास्थि-संस्थिता ।
अंकुशादि-प्रहरणा वरदादि-निषेविता ॥ 106 ॥

Mūlādhār'āmbuj'ārūḍhā pañca-vaktr'āsthi-samsthitā
aṅkuśādi-praharaṇā varadādi-niṣevitā

मुद्गौदनासक्त-चित्ता साकिन्यंबा-स्वरूपिणी ।
आज्ञा-चक्राब्ज-निलया शुक्लवर्णा षडानना ॥ 107 ॥

Mudg'audan'āsakta-cittā sākiny'ambā svarūpiṇī
ājñā-cakrābja-nilayā śukla-varṇā sad-ānanā

मज्जा-संस्था हंसवती-मुख्य-शक्ति-समन्विता ।
हरिद्रान्नैक-रसिका हाकिनी-रूप-धारिणी ॥ 108 ॥

Majjā-samsthā hamsavatī-mukhya-śakti-samanvitā
haridrān'n-aika-rasikā hākinī-rūpa-dhāriṇī

सहस्रदल-पद्मस्था सर्व-वर्णोप-शोभिता ।
सर्वायुध-धरा शुक्ल-संस्थिता सर्वतोमुखी ॥ 109 ॥

Sahasra-dala-padmasthā sarva-varṇ'opa-śobhitā
sarv'āyudha-dharā śukla-samsthitā sarvatomukhī

सर्वौदन-प्रीतचित्ता याकिन्यंबा-स्वरूपिणी ।
स्वाहा स्वधाऽमति-र्मेधा श्रुति-स्मृति-रनुत्तमा ॥ 110 ॥

Sarvaudana-prītacittā yākiny'ambā-svarūpiṇī
svāhā svadh'ā matir medhā śruti smṛtir anuttamā

पुण्यकीर्तिः पुण्यलभ्या पुण्यश्रवण-कीर्तना ।
पुलोमजार्चिता बन्धमोचनी बर्बरालका ॥ 111 ॥

Puṇya-kīrtiḥ puṇya-labhyā puṇya-śravaṇa-kīrtanā
pulomaj'ā arcitā bandha-mocanī barbarālakā

विमर्शरूपिणी विद्या वियदादि-जगत्प्रसूः ।
सर्वव्याधि-प्रशमनी सर्वमृत्यु-निवारिणी ॥ 112 ॥

Vimarśa-rūpiṇī vidyā viyad-ādi-jagat-prasūḥ
sarva-vyādhi-praśamanī sarva-mṛtyu-nivāriṇī

अग्रगण्या-ऽचिन्त्यरूपा कलिकल्मष-नाशिनी ।
कात्यायनी कालहन्त्री कमलाक्ष-निषेविता ॥ 113 ॥

Agragaṇy'ā cintya-rūpā kali-kalmaṣa-nāśinī
kātyāyanī kālahantrī kamalākṣa-niṣevitā

तांबूल-पूरित-मुखी दाडिमी-कुसुम-प्रभा ।
मृगाक्षी मोहिनी मुख्या मृडानी मित्ररूपिणी ॥ 114 ॥

Tāmbūla-pūrita-mukhī dāḍimī-kusuma-prabhā
mṛgākṣī mohinī mukhyā mṛḍānī mitra-rūpiṇī

नित्य-तृप्ता भक्तनिधि-र्नियन्त्री निखिलेश्वरी ।
मैत्र्यादि-वासनालभ्या महा-प्रलय-साक्षिणी ॥ 115 ॥

Nitya-tṛptā bhakta-nidhir niyantrī nikhileśvarī
maitryādi-vāsanālabhyā mahā-pralaya-sākṣiṇī

पराशक्तिः परानिष्ठा प्रज्ञानघन-रूपिणी ।
माध्वीपानालसा मत्ता मातृका-वर्ण-रूपिणी ॥ 116 ॥

Parāśaktiḥ parāniṣṭhā prajñāna-ghana-rūpiṇī
mādhvī-pān'ālasā mattā mātṛkā-varṇa-rūpiṇī

महाकैलास-निलया मृणाल-मृदु-दोर्लता ।
महनीया दयामूर्ति-र्महासाम्राज्य-शालिनी ॥ 117 ॥

Mahākailāsa-nilayā mṛṇāla-mṛdu-dorlatā
mahanīyā dayāmūrtir-mahā-sāmrājya-śālinī

आत्मविद्या महाविद्या श्रीविद्या कामसेविता ।
श्रीषोडशाक्षरीविद्या त्रिकूटा कामकोटिका ॥ 118 ॥

Ātmavidyā mahāvidyā śrīvidyā kāma-sevitā
śrī-ṣoḍaś'ākṣarī-vidyā trikūṭā kāma-koṭikā

कटाक्ष-किंकरी-भूत-कमला-कोटि-सेविता ।
शिरःस्थिता चन्द्रनिभा भालस्थेन्द्र-धनुः-प्रभा ॥ 119 ॥

Kaṭākṣa-kiṅkarī-bhūta-kamalā-koṭi-sevitā
śiraḥsthitā candra-nibhā bhālasth'endra-dhanuḥ-
prabhā

हृदयस्था रविप्रख्या त्रिकोणान्तर-दीपिका ।
दाक्षायणी दैत्यहन्त्री दक्षयज्ञविनाशिनी ॥ 120 ॥

Hṛdayasthā ravi-prakhyā trikoṇ'āntara-dīpikā
dākṣāyaṇī daitya-hantrī dakṣa-yajña-vināśinī

दरान्दोलित-दीर्घाक्षी दरहासोज्ज्वलन्मुखी ।
गुरु-मूर्ति-र्गुणनिधि-र्गोमाता गुहजन्म-भूः ॥ 121 ॥

Darāndolita-dīrghākṣī dara-hā'sojjvalan-mukhī
guru-mūrtir guṇanidhir gomātā guha-janma-bhūḥ

देवेशी दण्डनीतिस्था दहराकाश-रूपिणी ।
प्रतिपन्मुख्य-राकान्त-तिथि-मण्डल-पूजिता ॥ 122 ॥

Deveśī daṇḍa-nītisthā dahar'ākāśa-rūpiṇī
pratipan-mukhya-rākānta-tithi-maṇḍala-pūjitā

कलात्मिका कलानाथा काव्यालाप-विमोदिनी ।
सचामर-रमा-वाणी-सव्य-दक्षिण-सेविता ॥ 123 ॥

Kal'ātmikā kalā-nāthā kāvy'ālāpa-vimodinī
sacāmara-ramā-vāṇī-savya-dakṣiṇa-sevitā

आदिशक्ति-रमेयाऽऽत्मा परमा पावनाकृतिः ।
अनेक-कोटि-ब्रह्माण्ड-जननी दिव्य-विग्रहा ॥ 124 ॥

Ādiśaktir'amey'ātmā paramā pāvanākṛtiḥ
aneka-koṭi-brahmāṇḍa-jananī divya-vigrahā

क्लींकारी केवला गुह्या कैवल्य-पद-दायिनी ।
त्रिपुरा त्रिजगद्वन्द्या त्रिमूर्ति-स्त्रिदशेश्वरी ॥ 125 ॥

Klīmkārī kevalā guhyā kaivalya-pada-dāyinī
tripurā trijagad-vandyā trimūrtir tridaśeśvarī

त्र्यक्षरी दिव्य-गन्धाढ्या सिन्दूर-तिलकांचिता ।
उमा शैलेन्द्रतनया गौरी गन्धर्व-सेविता ॥ 126 ॥

Tryakṣarī divya-gandhāḍhyā sindūra-tilakāñcitā
umā śailendra-tanayā gaurī gandharva-sevitā

विश्वगर्भा स्वर्णगर्भा-ऽवरदा वागधीश्वरी ।
ध्यानगम्या-ऽपरिच्छेद्या ज्ञानदा ज्ञानविग्रहा ॥ 127 ॥

Viśva-garbhā svarṇa-garbhā avaradā vāg-adhīśvarī
dhyānagamy'āparicchedyā jñānadā jñāna-vigrahā

सर्व-वेदान्त-संवेद्या सत्यानन्द-स्वरूपिणी ।
लोपामुद्रार्चिता लीलाक्लृप्त-ब्रह्माण्ड-मण्डला ॥ 128 ॥

Sarva-vedānta-samvedyā saty'ānanda-svarūpiṇī
lopāmudr-ārcitā līlā'kḷpta-brahmāṇḍa-maṇḍalā

अदृश्या दृश्यरहिता विज्ञात्री वेद्य-वर्जिता ।
योगिनी योगदा योग्या योगानन्दा युगन्धरा ॥ 129 ॥

Adṛśyā dṛśya-rahitā vijñātrī vedya-varjitā
yoginī yogadā yogyā yog'ānandā yugandharā

इच्छाशक्ति-ज्ञानशक्ति-क्रियाशक्ति-स्वरूपिणी ।
सर्वाधारा सुप्रतिष्ठा सदसद्रूप-धारिणी ॥ 130 ॥

Icchāśakti-jñānaśakti-kriyāśakti-savrūpiṇī
sarvādhārā supratiṣṭhā sad-ạsad-rūpa-dhāriṇī

अष्टमूर्ति-रजाजेत्री लोकयात्रा-विधायिनी ।
एकाकिनी भूमरूपा निर्द्वैता द्वैतवर्जिता ॥ 131 ॥

Aṣṭamūrtir ajājetrī lokayātrā-vidhāyinī
ekākinī bhūmarūpā nirdvaitā dvaita-varjitā

अन्नदा वसुदा वृद्धा ब्रह्मात्मैक्य-स्वरूपिणी ।
बृहती ब्रह्माणी ब्राह्मी ब्रह्मानन्दा बलिप्रिया ॥ 132 ॥

Annadā vasudā vṛddhā brahm'ātmaikya-svarūpiṇī
bṛhatī brahmāṇī brāhmī brahm'ānandā balipriyā

भाषारूपा बृहत्सेना भावाभाव-विवर्जिता ।
सुखाराध्या शुभकरी शोभनासुलभागतिः ॥ 133 ॥

Bhāṣārūpā bṛhat-senā bhāv-ābhāva-vivarjitā
suk'ārādhyā śubhakarī śobhanā-sulabhā-gatiḥ

राजराजेश्वरी राज्यदायिनी राज्यवल्लभा ।
राजत्कृपा राजपीठ-निवेशित-निजाश्रिता ॥ 134 ॥

Rāja-rājeśvarī rājya-dāyinī rājya-vallabhā
rājat-kṛpā rāja-pīṭha-niveśita-nijāśritā

राज्यलक्ष्मीः कोशनाथा चतुरंग-बलेश्वरी ।
साम्राज्य- दायिनी सत्यसन्धा सागरमेखला ॥ 135 ॥

Rājyalakṣmīḥ kośanāthā caturaṅga-baleśvarī
sāmrājya-dāyinī satyasandhā sāgaramekhalā

दीक्षिता दैत्यशमनी सर्वलोकवशंकरी ।
सर्वार्थदात्री सावित्री सच्चिदानन्द-रूपिणी ॥ 136 ॥

Dīkṣitā daity'aśamanī sarva-loka-vaśaṅkarī
sarvārtha-dātrī sāvitrī sac-cidānanda-rūpiṇī

देशकालापरिच्छिन्ना सर्वगा सर्वमोहिनी ।
सरस्वती शास्त्रमयी गुहांबा गुह्यरूपिणी ॥ 137 ॥

Deśa-kālāparic-chinnā sarvagā sarva-mohinī
sarasvatī śāstramayī guhāmbā guhya'rūpiṇī

सर्वोपाधि-विनिर्मुक्ता सदाशिव-पतिव्रता ।
संप्रदायेश्वरी साध्वी गुरुमण्डल-रूपिणी ॥ 138 ॥

Sarv'opādhi-vinirmuktā sadāśiva-pativratā
sampradāy'eśvarī sādhvī guru-maṇḍala-rūpiṇī

कुलोत्तीर्णा भगाराध्या माया मधुमती मही ।
गणांबा गुह्यकाराध्या कोमलांगी गुरुप्रिया ॥ 139 ॥

Kulottīrṇā bhag'ārādhyā māyā madhumatī mahī
gaṇ'āmbā guhyak'ārādhyā komal'āṅgī gurupriyā

स्वतन्त्रा सर्वतन्त्रेशी दक्षिणामूर्ति-रूपिणी ।
सनकादि-समाराध्या शिवज्ञान-प्रदायिनी ॥ 140 ॥

Svatantrā sarva-tantreśī dakṣiṇā-mūrti-rūpiṇī
sanakādi-sam'ārādhyā śivajñāna-pradāyinī

चित्कलाऽऽनन्द-कलिका प्रेमरूपा प्रियंकरी ।
नामपारायण-प्रीता नन्दिविद्या नटेश्वरी ॥ 141 ॥

Citkal-ānanda-kalikā premarūpā priyamkarī
nāma-pārāyaṇa-prītā nandividyā naṭeśvarī

मिथ्या-जगदधिष्ठाना मुक्तिदा मुक्तिरूपिणी ।
लास्यप्रिया लयकरी लज्जा रंभादिवन्दिता ॥ 142 ॥

Mithyā jagad-adhiṣṭhānā muktidā muktirūpiṇī
lāsyapriyā layakarī lajjā rambhādi-vanditā

भवदाव-सुधावृष्टिः पापारण्य-दवानला ।
दौर्भाग्य-तूलवातूला जराध्वान्तरविप्रभा ॥ 143 ॥

Bhava-dāva-sudhā-vṛṣṭiḥ pāp'āraṇya-davānalā
daurbhāgya-tūlavātūlā jarā-dhvāntaraviprabhā

भाग्याब्धि-चन्द्रिका भक्त-चित्त-केकि-घनाघना ।
रोगपर्वत-दंभोलि-मृत्युदारु-कुठारिका ॥ 144 ॥

Bhāgy'ābdhi-candrikā bhakta-citta-keki-ghanā
ghanā
roga-parvata-dambholir-mṛtyu-dāru-kuṭhārikā

महेश्वरी महाकाली महाग्रासा महाशना ।
अपर्णा चण्डिका चण्डमुण्डासुर-निषूदिनी ॥ 145 ॥

Maheśvarī mahākalī mahāgrāsā mahāśanā
aparṇā caṇḍikā caṇḍa-muṇḍāsura-niṣūdinī

क्षराक्षरात्मिका सर्वलोकेशी विश्वधारिणी ।
त्रिवर्गदात्री सुभगा त्र्यंबका त्रिगुणात्मिका ॥ 146 ॥

Kṣar'ākṣar'ātmikā sarva-lokeśī viśva-dhāriṇī
trivarga-dātrī subhagā tryambakā triguṇ'ātmikā

स्वर्गापवर्गदा शुद्धा जपापुष्प-निभाकृतिः ।
ओजोवती द्युतिधरा यज्ञरूपा प्रियव्रता ॥ 147 ॥

Svarg'ā pavarga dā śuddhā japā-puṣpa-nibhākṛtiḥ
ojovatī dyuti-dharā yajña-rūpā priyavratā

दुराराध्या दुराधर्षा पाटली-कुसुम-प्रिया ।
महती मेरुनिलया मन्दार-कुसुम-प्रिया ॥ 148 ॥

Dur'ārādhyā dur'ādharṣā pāṭalī-kusuma-priyā
mahatī meru-nilayā mandāra-kusuma-priyā

वीराराध्या विराड्रूपा विरजा विश्वतोमुखी ।
प्रत्यग्-रूपा पराकाशा प्राणदा प्राणरूपिणी ॥ 149 ॥

Vīr'ārādhyā virāḍ-rūpā virajā viśvato-mukhī
pratyag-rūpā parākāśā prāṇadā prāṇa-rūpiṇī

मार्तण्ड-भैरवाराध्या मन्त्रिणी-न्यस्त-राज्यधूः ।
त्रिपुरेशी जयत्सेना निस्त्रैगुण्या परापरा ॥ 150 ॥

Mārtaṇda-bhairav'ārādhyā mantriṇī-nyasta-rājya-dhūḥ
tripureśī jayatsenā nistraiguṇyā parāparā

सत्यज्ञानानन्द-रूपा सामरस्य-परायणा ।
कपर्दिनी कलामाला कामधुक्काम-रूपिणी ॥ 151 ॥

Satya'jñ'ānānanda-rūpā sāmarasya parāyaṇā
kapardinī kalāmālā kāmadhuk kāma-rūpiṇī

कलानिधिः काव्यकला रसज्ञा रसशेवधिः ।
पुष्टा पुरातना पूज्या पुष्करा पुष्करेक्षणा ॥ 152 ॥

Kalā-nidhiḥ kāvya-kalā rasajñā rasa-śevadhiḥ
puṣṭā purātanā pūjyā puṣkarā puṣkar'ekṣaṇa

परंज्योतिः परंधाम परमाणुः परात्परा ।
पाशहस्ता पाशहन्त्री परमन्त्र-विभेदिनी ॥ 153 ॥

Param-jyotiḥ param-dhāma param'āṇuḥ parāt-parā
pāśa-hastā pāśa-hantrī para-mantra-vibhedinī

मूर्ताऽमूर्ता ऽनित्यतृप्ता मुनिमानस-हंसिका ।
सत्यव्रता सत्यरूपा सर्वान्तर्यामिनी सती ॥ 154 ॥

Mūrt'amūrt'ānitya- tṛptā muni-mānasa-hamsikā
satyavratā sātyarūpā sarv'āntaryāmiṇī satī

ब्रह्माणी ब्रह्मजननी बहुरूपा बुधार्चिता ।
प्रसवित्री प्रचण्डाऽऽज्ञा प्रतिष्ठा प्रकटाकृतिः ॥ 155 ॥

Brahmāṇī brahma-jananī bahu-rūpā budh'ārcitā
prasavitrī pracaṇḍājñā pratiṣṭhā prakaṭākṛtiḥ

प्राणेश्वरी प्राणदात्री पंचाशत्पीठं-रूपिणी ।
विशृंखला विविक्तस्था वीरमाता वियत्प्रसूः ॥ 156 ॥

Prāṇeśvarī prāṇa-dātrī pañcāśat-pīṭha-rūpiṇī
viśṛṅkhalā viviktasthā vīra-mātā viyat-prasūḥ

मुकुन्दा मुक्तिनिलया मूलविग्रह-रूपिणी ।
भावज्ञा भवरोगघ्नी भवचक्र-प्रवर्तिनी ॥ 157 ॥

Mukundā mukti-nilayā mūla-vigraha-rūpiṇī
bhāvajñā bhava-rogaghnī bhava-cakra-pravartinī

छन्दःसारा शास्त्रसारा मन्त्रसारा तलोदरी ।
उदारकीर्ति-रुद्दामवैभवा वर्णरूपिणी ॥ 158 ॥

Chandaḥ-sārā śāstra-sārā mantra-sārā talodarī
udāra-kīrtir uddāma-vaibhavā varṇarūpiṇī

जन्ममृत्यु-जरातप्त-जन-विश्रान्ति-दायिनी ।
सर्वोपनिषदुद्घुष्टा शान्त्यतीत-कलात्मिका ॥ 159 ॥

Janma-mṛtyu-jarā-tapta-jana-viśrānti-dāyinī
sarv'opaniṣad-udghuṣṭā śānty'atīta-kalātmikā

गंभीरा गगनान्तस्था गर्विता गानलोलुपा ।
कल्पना-रहिता काष्ठाऽकान्ता कान्तार्ध-विग्रहा ॥ 160 ॥

Gambhīrā gaganāntasthā garvitā gānalolupā
kalpanā-rahitā kāṣṭh'ākāntā kānt-ārdha-vigrahā

कार्यकारण-निर्मुक्ता कामकेली-तरंगिता ।
कनत्कनक-ताटंका लीला-विग्रह-धारिणी ॥ 161 ॥

Kārya-kārana nirmuktā kāmakeli-taramgitā
kanat-kanaka-tāṭaṅkā līlā-vigraha-dhāriṇī

अजा क्षयविनिर्मुक्ता मुग्धा क्षिप्र-प्रसादिनी ।
अन्तर्मुख-समाराध्या बहिर्मुख-सुदुर्लभा ॥ 162 ॥

Ajā kṣaya-vinirmuktā mugdhā kṣipra-prasādinī
antar-mukha-samārādhyā bahir-mukha-sudur labhā

त्रयी त्रिवर्ग-निलया त्रिस्था त्रिपुर-मालिनी ।
निरामया निरालंबा स्वात्मारामा सुधासृतिः ॥ 163 ॥

Trayī trivarga-nilayā tristhā tripura-mālinī
nirāmayā nirālambā svātm'ārāmā sudhās'ṛtiḥ

संसारपंक-निर्मग्न-समुद्धरण-पण्डिता ।
यज्ञप्रिया यज्ञकर्त्री यजमान-स्वरूपिणी ॥ 164 ॥

Samsāra-paṅka-nirmagna-samuddharaṇa-paṇḍitā
yajñpriyā yajñakartrī yajamāna-svarūpiṇī

धर्माधारा धनाध्यक्षा धनधान्य-विवर्धिनी ।
विप्रप्रिया विप्ररूपा विश्वभ्रमण-कारिणी ।। 165 ।।

Dharmādhārā dhan'ādhyakṣā dhana-dhānya-vivardhinī
vipra-priyā vipra-rūpā viśva-bhramaṇa-kāriṇī

विश्वग्रासा विद्रुमाभा वैष्णवी विष्णुरूपिणी ।
अयोनि-र्योनि-निलया कूटस्था कुलरूपिणी ।। 166 ।।

Viśva-grāsā vidrum'ābhā vaiṣṇavī viṣṇu-rūpiṇī
ayonir yoni-nilayā kūṭasthā kularūpiṇī

वीरगोष्ठी-प्रिया वीरा नैष्कर्म्या नादरूपिणी ।
विज्ञानकलना कल्या विदग्धा बैन्दवासना ।। 167 ।।

Vīragoṣṭhī-priyā vīrā naiṣkarmyā nādarūpiṇī
vijñāna-kalanā kalyā vidagdhā baindav'āsanā

तत्त्वाधिका तत्त्वमयी तत्त्वमर्थ-स्वरूपिणी ।
सामगान-प्रिया सोम्या सदाशिव-कुटुंबिनी ।। 168 ।।

Tattvādhikā tattvamayī tattvamartha-svarūpiṇī
sāmagāna-priyā somyā sadāśiva-kuṭumbinī

सव्यापसव्य-मार्गस्था सर्वापद्विनिवारिणी ।
स्वस्था स्वभावमधुरा धीरा धीरसमर्चिता ।। 169 ।।

Savy'āpasavya-mārgasthā sarv'āpad-vinivāriṇī
svasthā svabhāva-madhurā dhīrā dhīra-samarcitā

चैतन्यार्घ्य-समाराध्या चैतन्य-कुसुम-प्रिया ।
सदोदिता सदातुष्टा तरुणादित्य-पाटला ॥ 170 ॥

Caitany'ārghya-samārādhyā caitanya-kusuma-priyā
sad-oditā sadā-tuṣṭā taruṇ-āditya-pāṭalā

दक्षिणा-दक्षिणाराध्या दरस्मेर-मुखांबुजा ।
कौलिनी-केवलाऽनर्घ्य-कैवल्य-पद-दायिनी ॥ 171 ॥

Dakṣiṇā-adakṣiṇārādhyā darasmera-mukhāmbujā
kaulinī-keva'lānarghya kaivalya-pada-dāyinī

स्तोत्र-प्रिया स्तुतिमती श्रुति-संस्तुत-वैभवा ।
मनस्विनी मानवती महेशी मंगलाकृतिः ॥ 172 ॥

Stotra-priyā stutimatī śruti-samstuta-vaibhavā
manasvinī mānavatī maheśī maṅgal'ākṛtiḥ

विश्वमाता जगद्धात्री विशालाक्षी विरागिणी ।
प्रगल्भा परमोदारा परामोदा मनोमयी ॥ 173 ॥

Viśvamātā jagad-dhātrī viśalākṣī virāgiṇī
pragalbhā param'odārā parāmodā manomayī

व्योमकेशी विमानस्था वज्रिणी वामकेश्वरी ।
पंचयज्ञ-प्रिया पंचप्रेत-मंचाधिशायिनी ॥ 174 ॥

Vyomakeśī vimānasthā vajriṇī vāmakeśvarī
pañca-yajña-priyā pañca-preta-mañc'ādhiśāyinī

पंचमी पंचभूतेशी पंचसंख्योपचारिणी ।
शाश्वती शाश्वतैश्वर्या शर्मदा शंभुमोहिनी ॥ 175 ॥

Pañcamī pañcabhūteśī pañca-saṅkhyopacāriṇī
śāśvatī śāśvat-aiśvaryā śarmadā śambhu-mohinī

धरा धरसुता धन्या धर्मिणी धर्मवर्धिनी ।
लोकातीता गुणातीता सर्वातीता शमात्मिका ॥ 176 ॥

Dharā-dhara-sutā dhanyā dharmiṇī dharma-vardhinī
lok'ātītā guṇ'ātītā sarv'ātītā śam'ātmikā

बन्धूक-कुसुम-प्रख्या बाला लीला-विनोदिनी ।
सुमंगली सुखकरी सुवेषाढ्या सुवासिनी ॥ 177 ॥

Bandhūka-kusuma-prakhyā bālā līlā-vinodinī
sumaṅgalī sukhakarī suveṣāḍhyā suvāsinī

सुवासिन्यर्चन-प्रीताऽऽशोभना शुद्ध-मानसा ।
बिन्दु-तर्पण-सन्तुष्टा पूर्वजा त्रिपुरांबिका ॥ 178 ॥

Suvāsinyarcana-prītā'-śobhanā śuddha'mānasā
bindu-tarpaṇa-santuṣṭā pūrvajā tripur'āmbikā

दशमुद्रा-समाराध्या त्रिपुराश्रीवशंकरी ।
ज्ञानमुद्रा ज्ञानगम्या ज्ञान-ज्ञेय-स्वरूपिणी ॥ 179 ॥

Daśamudrā-samārādhyā tripurāśrī-vaśamkarī
jñāna-mudrā jñāna-gamyā jñana-jñeya-svarūpiṇī

योनिमुद्रा त्रिखण्डेशी त्रिगुणांबा त्रिकोणगा ।
अनघाऽद्भुत-चारित्रा वांछितार्थ-प्रदायिनी ॥ 180 ॥

Yonimudrā trikhaṇḍeśī triguṇ'āmbā trikoṇagā
anagh'ādbhuta-cāritrā vāñchitārtha-pradāyinī

अभ्यासातिशय-ज्ञाता षडध्वातीत-रूपिणी ।
अव्याज-करुणा-मूर्ति-रज्ञान-ध्वान्त-दीपिका ॥ 181 ॥

Abhyās-ātiśaya-jñātā ṣaḍadhv'ātīta-rūpiṇī
avyāja-karuṇā-mūrtir ajñāna-dhvānta-dīpikā

आबाल-गोप-विदिता सर्वानुल्लंध्य-शासना ।
श्रीचक्रराज-निलया श्रीमत्-त्रिपुरसुन्दरी ॥ 182 ॥

Ābāla-gopa-viditā sarv'ānullaṅghya-śāsanā
śrīcakrarāja-nilayā śrīmat-tripurasundarī

श्रीशिवा शिव-शक्त्यैक्य-रूपिणी ललितांबिका ॥ ओं ॥
(इति श्री ब्रह्माण्डपुराणे उत्तरखण्डे
श्री हयग्रीवागस्त्य-संवादे
श्री ललितासहस्रनाम-स्तोत्र-कथनं संपूर्णम्)

Śrī-śivā śiva-śaktyaikya-rūpiṇī lalit'āmbika //om//

(Iti śri brahmāṇḍapurāṇe uttarakhaṇḍe śri
hayagrīvāgastya saṁvāde
śri lalitāsahasranāma stotra-kathanaṁ sampūrṇam)

॥ श्री ललिता-सहस्र-नामावलिः ॥

//*Śrī Lalitā-sahasra-nāmāvaliḥ*//

1. ओं श्रीमात्रे नमः

Om Śrī - mātre namah

Salutations to the Divine Mother, who is the Mother of all.

2. ओं श्रीमहाराज्ञ्यै नमः

Om Srī - mahā - rājñyai namah

Salutations to the great Empress of the whole Universe.

3. ओं श्रीमत्सिंहासनेश्वर्यै नमः

Om Śrīmat - simhāsan'eśvaryai namah

Salutations to the great Sovereign enthroned on the lion's back.

4. ओं चिदग्नि - कुण्ड - सम्भूतायै नमः

Om cid - agni - kunda - sambhūtāyai namah

Salutations to Her who came out of the fire of Pure Consciousness.

5. ओं देवकार्य - समुद्यतायै नमः

Om deva - kārya - samudyatāyai namaḥ

Salutations to Her who ever promotes the cause of Divine forces.

6. ओं उद्यद्भानु - सहस्राभायै नमः

Om udyad - bhānu - sahasrābhāyai namaḥ

Salutations to Her who is radiant as a thousand suns rising together.

7. ओं चतुर्बाहु - समन्वितायै नमः

Om catur - bāhu - samanvitāyai namah

Salutations to the four - armed Divinity.

8. ओं रागस्वरूप - पाशाढ्यायै नमः

Om rāga - svarūpa - pāśādhyāyai namaḥ

Salutations to Her who holds in her lower left hand a noose representing the power of love.

9. ओं क्रोधाकाराङ्कुशोज्ज्वलायै नमः

Om krodhā - kar'āṅkuś' ojjvalāyai namaḥ

Salutations to Her holding the flashing Aṅkuśa (goad) of anger in Her lower right hand for restraining the forces of evil.

10. ओं मनोरूपेक्षु - कोदण्डायै नमः

Om mano - rūp'ekṣu - kodaṇḍāyai namaḥ

Salutations to Her who wields in her upper left hand a Sugarcane bow that stands for mind.

11. ओं पञ्चतन्मात्र - सायकायै नमः

Om pañca - tanmātra - sāyakāyai namaḥ

Salutations to Her who holds five arrows representing the five Tanmātras (subtle elements).

12. ओं निजारुण - प्रभापूर - मज्जद्ब्रह्माण्ड - मण्डलायै नमः

Om nij'āruṇa - prabhā - pūra - majjad - brahmāṇḍa - maṇḍalāyai namaḥ

Salutations to Her in the rosy splendour of whose form the whole universe is bathed.

13. ओं चम्पकाशोक-पुन्नाग-सौगन्धिक-लसत्कचायै नमः

Om campak'āśoka - punnāga - saugandhika - lasat - kacāyai namaḥ

Salutations to Her whose shining locks of hair impart their fragrance to flowers like Campaka, Aśoka and Punnāga adorning them.

14. ओं कुरुविन्दमणि - श्रेणी - कनत्कोटीर - मण्डितायै नमः

Om kuruvinda - maṇi - śreṇī - kanat - koṭīra - maṇḍitāyai namaḥ

Salutations to Her whose crown is shining with rows of Kuruvinda gems.

15. ओं अष्टमीचन्द्र - विभ्राज - दलिकस्थल - शोभितायै नमः

Om aṣṭamī - candra - vibhrājadalika - sthala - śobhitāyai namaḥ

Salutations to Her whose forehead shines, arching like the crescent moon of the eighth lunar digit (Aṣṭamī).

16. ओं मुखचन्द्र - कलङ्काभ - मृगनाभि - विशेषकायै नमः

Om mukha - candra - kalaṅkābha mṛganābhi - viśeṣakāyai namaḥ

Salutations to Her whose moon - like face is distinguished by the Kastūri Tilaka like the spot in the moon.

17. ओं वदनस्मर - माङ्गल्य - गृहतोरण - चिल्लिकायै नमः

Om vadana - smara - māṅgalya - gṛha - toraṇa - cillikāyai namaḥ

Salutations to Her whose face, the auspicious home of Kāma (Cupid), has eyebrows that resemble archways leading to that abode of beauty.

18. ओं वक्त्रलक्ष्मी-परीवाह-चलन्मीनाभ-लोचनायै नमः

Om vaktra - lakṣmī - parīvāha - calan - mīnābha - locanāyai namaḥ

Salutations to Her whose eyes move like fish in the streams of beauty flowing from Her face.

19. ओं नवचम्पक - पुष्पाभ - नासादण्ड - विराजितायै नमः

Om nava campaka - puṣpābha - nāsā - daṇḍa - virā - jitāyai namaḥ

Salutations to Her whose shapely nose is like a fresh - blown Campaka bud.

20. ओं ताराकान्ति - तिरस्कारि - नासाभरण - भासुरायै नमः

Om tārā - kānti - tiraskāri - nāsābharaṇa - bhāsurāyai namaḥ

Salutations to Her with a nasal ornament set with a jewel that excels the brilliance of the planet Venus.

21. ओं कदम्बमञ्जरी - क्लृप्त - कर्णपूर - मनोहरायै नमः

Om kadamba - mañjarī - klpta - karṇapūra manoharāyai namaḥ

Salutations to Her who is radiant and charming with a bunch of Kadamba flowers over her ears.

22. ओं ताटङ्क - युगली - भूत - तपनोडुप - मण्डलायै नमः

Om tāṭaṅka - yugalī - bhūta - tapan'oḍupa - maṇḍalāyai namaḥ

Salutations to Her who has the orbs of the sun and the moon as Her pair of ear pendants.

23. ओं पद्मरागशिलादर्श - परिभावि - कपोलभुवे नमः

Om padma - rāga - śil'ādarśa - paribhāvi kapola - bhuve namaḥ

Salutations to Her whose cheeks are far fairer than mirrors of ruby (Padmarāga).

24. ओं नवविद्रुम - बिम्बश्री - न्यक्कारि - रदनच्छदायै नमः

Om nava - vidruma - bimba - śrī - nyakkāri - radana - cchādāyai namaḥ

Salutations to Her whose lips outshine the redness of fresh coral and bimba fruit.

25. ओं शुद्धविद्यांकुराकार - द्विजपंक्ति - द्वयोज्ज्वलायै नमः

Om śuddha - vidyā'ṅkurākāra - dvija - paṅkti - dvay'ojjvalāyai namaḥ

Salutations to Her whose beauty is enhanced by her rows of teeth that resemble the sprouting of pure Knowledge (Śuddha - Vidyā or Śrī - Vidyā).

26. ओं कर्पूरवीटिकामोद - समाकर्षि - दिगन्तरायै नमः

Om Karpūra - vīṭik'āmoda - samākarṣi - digantarāyai namaḥ

Salutations to Her, the fragrance of the campho limbedded betel roll in whose mouth is spreading in all directions.

27. ओं निज-सल्लाप-माधुर्यु-विनिर्भत्स्ति-कच्छप्यै नमः

Om nija - sallāpa - mādhurya - vinirbhartsita - kacchapyai namaḥ

Salutations to Her whose speech is more melodious than the Veeṇa of Sarasvatī known as Kacchapi.

28. ओं मन्दस्मित - प्रभापूर - मज्जत्कामेश - मानसायै नमः

Om manda - smita - prabhā - pūra - majjat - kāmeśa - mānasāyai namaḥ

Salutations to Her the radiance of whose smile inundates the mind of Kāmeśvara, Her Consort.

29. ओं अनाकलित - सादृश्य - चिबुकश्री - विराजितायै नमः

Om anākalita - sādṛśya - cibuka - śrī - virājitāyai namaḥ

Salutations to Her whose chin is peerless in beauty.

30. ओं कामेश-बद्ध-मांगल्य-सूत्र-शोभित-कन्धरायै नमः

Om Kāmeśa - baddha - māṅgalya - sūtra - śobhita - kandharāyai namaḥ

Salutations to Her whose neck is adorned with the Maṅgalasūtra (marriage thread) fastened thereon by Her consort Kāmeśvara.

31. ओं कनकांगद - केयूर - कमनीय - भुजान्वितायै नमः

Om kanak'āṅgada - keyūra - kamanīya - bhuj'ān - vitāyai namaḥ

Salutations to Her whose beautiful arms are decked with armlets and bracelets of gold.

32. ओं रत्नग्रैवेय-चिन्ताक-लोल-मुक्ता-फलान्वितायै नमः

Om ratna - graiveya - cintāka - lola - muktāphal'ān - vitāyai namaḥ

Salutations to Her who wears a gem - set necklace having a big pearl as a pendant.

33. ओं कामेश्वर - प्रेमरत्न - मणि - प्रतिपण - स्तन्यै नमः

Om kāmeśvara - prema - ratna - maṇi - pratipaṇa - stanyai namaḥ

Salutations to Her whose breasts form the price she pays to Her Consort (Maheśvara) in return for the gem of love He bestows on Her.

34. ओं नाभ्यालवाल-रोमालि-लता-फल-कुचद्वय्यै नमः

Om nābhy'ālavāla - romāli - latā - phala - kuca - dvayyai namaḥ

Salutations to Her whose breasts look like fruits on the creeper of the hair - line spreading upwards from the navel.

35. ओं लक्ष्यरोम - लताधारता - समुन्नेय - मध्यमायै नमः

Om lakṣya - roma - latā - dhāratā- samunneya - madhyamāyai namaḥ

Salutations to Her who has a waist so slender that it can only be inferred as a base for the creeper of fine hair springing from her navel upwards.

36. ओं स्तनभार - दलन्मध्य - पट्टबन्ध - वलित्रयायै नमः

Om stana - bhāra dalan - madhya - paṭṭa - bandha - vali - trayāyai namaḥ

Salutations to Her whose waist, breaking under the weight of Her breasts, gets a supporting belt in the three folds of Her abdomen.

37. ओं अरुणारुणकौसुंभ - वस्त्र - भास्वत् - कटीतट्यै नमः

Oṁ aruṇ'aruṇa - kaụsumbha - vastra- bhāsvat - kaṭī - taṭyai namaḥ

Salutations to Her who wears a garment of deep red round Her hip.

38. ओं रत्न-किंकिणिका-रम्य-रशना-दाम-भूषितायै मनः

Om ratna - kiṅkiṇik'āramya - raśanā - dāma - bhūṣitāyai namaḥ

Salutations to Her who is adorned with a girdle having many mini bells set with precious stones.

39. ओं कामेश-ज्ञात-सौभाग्य-मार्दवोरु-द्वयान्वितायै नमः

Om kāmeśa - jñāta - saubhāgya - mārdav'oru - dvay'ānvitāyai namaḥ

Salutations to Her the beauty and smoothness of whose thighs are known only to Her consort, the Conqueror of Love (Kameśa)

40. ओं माणिक्य - मुकुटाकार - जानुद्वय - विराजितायै नमः

Om māṇikya - mukuṭ'ākāra jānu - dvaya - virājitāyai namaḥ

Salutations to Her whose two knees are like crowns shaped from the precious stone Māṇikya.

41. ओं इन्द्रगोप - परिक्षिप्तस्मरतूणाभ - जंघिकायै नम:

Om indra - gopa - parikṣipta - smara - tūṇābha - jaṅghikāyai namaḥ

Salutations to Her whose calf - muscles resemble the quiver of the god of love with bright glow - worm - like decorations.

42. ओं गूढगुल्फायै नम:

Om gūḍha - gulphāyai namaḥ

Salutations to Her whose ankles are well - filled and therefore without protrusion.

43. ओं कूर्मपृष्ठ - जयिष्णु - प्रपदान्वितायै नम:

Om kūrma - pṛṣṭha - jayiṣṇu-
prapad'ānvitāyai namaḥ

Salutations to Her the arch of whose feet rivals the shapeliness and beauty of the back of a tortoise.

44. ओं नखदीधिति - संछन्न - नमज्जन - तमोगुणायै नम:

Om nakha - dīdhiti - samchanna - namajjana - tamo - guṇāyai namaḥ

Salutations to Her the illumining splendour of whose toe nails dispels the darkness of ignorance in the votaries prostrating at Her feet.

45. ओं पदद्वय - प्रभाजाल - पराकृत - सरोरुहायै नमः

Om pada - dvaya - prabhā - jāla - parākṛta - saroruhāyai namaḥ

Salutations to Her whose feet defeat the lotus in beauty.

46. ओं सिञ्जान - मणिमञ्जीर - मण्डित - श्रीपदाम्बुजायै नमः

Om siñjāna - maṇi - mañjīra - maṇḍita - śrīpad'āmbujāyai namaḥ

Salutations to Her whose lotus - feet are adorned with tinkling anklets set with jewels.

47. ओं मराली - मन्दगमनायै नमः

Om marālī - manda - gamanāyai namaḥ

Salutations to Her whose gait is slow and gentle like the swan's.

48. ओं महालावण्य - शेवधये नमः

Om mahā - lāvaṇya - śevadhaye namaḥ

Salutations to Her who is a treasure house of Divine beauty.

49. ओं सर्वारुणायै नमः

Om sarv'āruṇāyai namaḥ

Salutations to Her who is rose - hued all over.

50. ओं अनवद्याङ्ग्यै नमः

Om anavadyā'ṅgyai namaḥ

Salutations to Her who is faultless in every limb.

51. ओं सर्वाभरण - भूषितायै नमः

Om Sarv'ābharaṇa - bhūṣitāyai namaḥ

Salutations to Her who is adorned with divine ornaments.

52. ओं शिव - कामेश्वरांकस्थायै नमः

Om śiva - kāmeśvar'āṅkasthāyai namaḥ

Salutations to Her who is seated on the lap of Śiva, the conqueror of desire (Kāmeśvara).

53. ओं शिवायै नमः

Om śivāyai namaḥ

Salutations to Her, the Consort of Śiva, whose Power She is.

54. ओं स्वाधीन - वल्लभायै नमः

Om svādhīna - vallabhāyai namaḥ

Salutations to Her who dominates over Her Consort Śiva in the creative part of the cyclic motion of time.

55. ओं सुमेरु - मध्य - शृंगस्थायै नमः

Om sumeru - madhya - śṛṅga - sthāyai namaḥ

Salutations to Her who dwells on the mid - most peak of Mount Meru.

56. ओं श्रीमन्नगर - नायिकायै नमः

Om śrīman - nagara - nāyikāyai namaḥ

Salutations to Her who is the Bindu, the central circle of bliss in the Śrī - cakra.

57. ओं चिन्तामणिगृहान्तस्थायै नमः

Om cintāmaṇi - gṛh'āntasthāyai namaḥ

Salutations to Her whose abode is Maṇidvīpa the Island of Wish-yielding Gem.

58. ओं पंच - ब्रह्मासन - स्थितायै नमः

Om pañca - brahm'āsana - sthitāyai namaḥ

Salutations to Her who rests on a seat formed of the five Divinities (Brahmans) – Brahmā, Viṣṇu, Rudra, Īśāna and Sadāśiva.

59. ओं महापद्माटवी - संस्थायै नमः

Om mahā - padm'āṭavī - samsthāyai namaḥ

Salutations to Her who dwells in a lotus forest – the thousand - petalled lotus of the Sahasrāra.

60. ओं कदंबवन - वासिन्यै नमः

Om kadamba - vana - vāsinyai namaḥ

Salutations to Her who resides amidst a grove of Kadamba trees (which fringe the Maṇidvīpa).

61. ओं सुधासागर - मध्यस्थायै नमः

Om sudhā - sāgara - madhyasthāyai namaḥ

Salutations to Her who dwells in the centre of the sea of Nectar (which is the light of the Blissful Moon of the pericap of the Sahasrāra).

62. ओं कामाक्ष्यै नमः

Om kāmākyyai namaḥ

Salutations to Her the look of whose eyes is full of grace.

63. ओं कामदायिन्यै नमः

Om kāma - dāyinyai namaḥ

Salutations to Her who grants all the prayers of votaries.

64. ओं देवर्षि - गण - संघात - स्तूयमानात्म - वैभवायै नमः

Om devarṣi - gaṇa - saṅghāta- stūyamān'ātma - vaibhavāyai namaḥ

Salutations to Her whose majesty is the subject of praise of hosts of sages and divine beings.

65. ओं भण्डासुर-वधोद्युक्त-शक्तिसेना-समन्वितायै नमः

Om bhaṇḍ'āsura - vadho'dyukta -śakti- senā - saman - vitāyai namaḥ

Salutations to Her under whose command an army of Śaktis are intent on destroying Bhaṇḍāsura (the Asura being Ignorance, Lalitāmbikā, the Atman, and the Śaktis, the potencies of the Atman.)

66. ओं संपत्करी - समारूढ - सिंधुर - व्रज - सेवितायै नमः

Om sampatkarī - samārūḍha - sindhura - vraja - sevitāyai namaḥ

Salutations to Her who is accompanied by a regiment of elephants headed by Sampatkarī.

67. ओं अश्वारूढाधिष्ठिताश्व-कोटि-कोटिभि-रावृतायै नमः

Om aśvārūḍh'ādhiṣṭhit'āśva - koṭi - koṭibhir - āvṛtāyai namaḥ

Salutations to Her who is surrounded by a cavalry of several crores of horses under the command of Aśvārūḍhā.

68. ओं चक्रराज - रथारूढ - सर्वायुध - परिष्कृतायै नमः

Om cakra - rāja - rath'ārūḍha - sarv'āyudha - pariṣkṛtāyai namaḥ

Salutations to Her seated in Her chariot Cakra - rāja equipped with armaments of every kind.

69. ओं गेयचक्र - रथारूढ - मंत्रिणी - परिसेवितायै नमः

Om geya - cakra - rath'ārūḍha - mantriṇī pari - sevitāyai namaḥ

Salutations to Her who is attended by Her minister (Śyāmalā) seated in Her chariot named Geya - cakra.

70. ओं किरिचक्र - रथारूढ - दण्डनाथा - पुरस्कृतायै नमः

Om kiri - cakra - rath'ārūḍha - daṇḍa - nāthā puras - kṛtāyai namaḥ

Salutations to Her who is preceded by Daṇḍanātha, the commander of Her armies in his chariot Kiri - cakra.

71. ओं ज्वालामालिनिकाक्षिप्त - वह्निप्राकार - मध्यगायै नमः

Om jvālā - mālinik'ākṣipta - vahni - prākāra - madhya - gāyai namaḥ

Salutations to Her who has taken position

in the centre of the rampart of fire constructed by Jvālāmālinikā.

72. ओं भण्डसैन्य - वधोद्युक्त - शक्ति - विक्रम - हर्षितायै नमः

Om bhanda - sainya - vadh'odyukta - śakti - vikrama - harṣitāyai namaḥ

Salutations to Her who rejoices at the valour of Her Śaktis bent on destroying the army of Bhaṇḍa.

73. ओं नित्या - पराक्रमाटोप - निरीक्षण - समुत्सुकायै नमः

Om nityā - parākram'ātopa - nirīkṣana samutsukāyai namaḥ

Salutations to Her who is delighted on seeing the aggressiveness of Her Nityā deities in their attack on the army of Bhanda.

74. ओं भण्डपुत्र-वधोद्युक्त-बाला-विक्रम-नन्दितायै नमः

Om bhanda - putra - vadh'odyukta - bālā - vikrama - nanditāyai namaḥ

Salutations to Her who is overjoyed to see Her daughter Bālā who is intent on slaying the son of Bhaṇḍa.

75. ओं मन्त्रिण्यंबा-विरचित-विषंग-वध-तोषितायै नमः

Om mantriṇy'ambā - viracita - visaṅga - vadha - toṣitāyai namaḥ

Salutations to Her who feels satisfaction at the destruction of Viṣaṅga by Her chief minister Śyāmalā.

76. ओं विशुक्र - प्राणहरण - वाराही - वीर्य - नंदितायै नमः

Om viśukra - prāṇa - haraṇa - vārāhī - vīrya nanditāyai namaḥ

Salutations to Her who appreciates the prowess displayed by Vārāhī in the destruction of Viśukra.

77. ओं कामेश्वर - मुखालोक - कल्पित - श्रीगणेश्वरायै नमः

Om kāmeśvara - mukh'āloka - kalpita - śrī - gaṇeśvarāyai namaḥ

Salutations to Her who by a mere glance at her Consort Maheśvara generates Śrī Gaṇeśa (the elephant headed deity).

78. ओं महागणेश - निर्भिन्न - विघ्नयन्त्र - प्रहर्षितायै नमः

Om mahā - gaṇeśa - nirbhinna - vighna - Yantra - prahar - ṣitāyai namaḥ

Salutations to Her who rejoices when that Gaṇeśa destroys the magical devices placed by Bhaṇḍāsura as obstacles to Her victory.

79. ओं भण्डासुरेन्द्र - निर्मुक्त - शस्त्र - प्रत्यस्त्र - वर्षिण्यै नमः

Om bhaṇḍāsur'endra - nirmukta - śastra

pratyastra - varṣinyai namaḥ

Salutations to Her who counters by Her own missiles the rain of missiles directed against Her by Bhandāsura.

80. ओं करांगुलि - नखोत्पन्न - नारायण - दशाकृत्यै नमः

Om karāṅguli - nakh'otpanna - nārāyana - daśākrtyai namaḥ

Salutations to Her who out of Her finger nails recreated all the ten Incarnations of Visnu to destroy the Asuras slain by Him in His incarnations and now recreated magically by Bhanda out of a missile of his.

81. ओं महा - पाशुपतास्त्राग्नि - निर्दग्धासुर - सैनिकायै नमः

Om mahā - pāśupat'āstr'āgni - nirdagdh'ā sura - sainikāyai namah

Salutations to Her who burned to death the armies of demons with the fire of the great missile pāśupata.

82. ओं कामेश्वरास्त्र - निर्दग्ध - सभण्डासुर - शून्यकायै नमः

Om kāmeśvar'āstra - nirdagdha sabhand'āsura - *śūnyakāyai namaḥ*

Salutations to Her who with the flames of the missile Kāmeśvara caused the destruction of Bhaṇḍa and also of his Capital Śūnyaka.

83. ओं ब्रह्मोपेन्द्र - महेन्द्रादि - देव - संस्तुत - वैभवायै नमः

Om brahm'opendra - mahendrādi - deva - samstuta - vaibhavāyai namaḥ

Salutations to Her whose manifold powers (displayed in the fight with Bhaṇḍa) are praised by Brahmā, Viṣṇu and Indra.

84. ओं हर - नेत्राग्नि - संदग्ध - काम - संजीवनौषध्यै नमः

Om hara - netr'āgni - sandagdha - kāma - sañjīvan'auṣadhyai namaḥ

Salutations to Her, the life giving herb, that revived the god of love (Kāma - deva) who had been burnt to death by the fire of Śiva's eyes.

85. ओं श्रीमद्वाग्भव - कूटैक - स्वरूप - मुख - पंकजायै नमः

Om Śrīmad - vāgbhava - kūṭ'aika - svarūpa - mukha - paṅkajāyai namaḥ

Salutations to Her whose lotus face represents the Vāgbhava - Kūṭa of the pañca -daśākṣarī - mantra which is the subtle form of the Devi.

86. ओं कण्ठाधः-कटि-पर्यन्त-मध्यकूट-स्वरूपिण्यै नमः

Om Kaṇṭhādhaḥ - kaṭi - paryanta - madhya - kūṭa - svarūpiṇyai namaḥ

Salutations to Her whose middle region from the neck to the waist is represented by the central part (Kāmarāja - Kūṭa) of the same Mantra.

87. ओं शक्तिकूटैकतापन्न - कट्यधोभाग - धारिण्यै नमः

Om śakti - kūṭ'aikat'āpanna - kaṭyadho - bhāga - dhāriṇyai namaḥ

Salutations to Her whose form below waist is identical with the last part (Śakti - Kūṭa) of Pañca - daś'ākṣarī Mantra.

88. ओं मूलमन्त्रात्मिकायै नमः

Om mūla - mantr'ātmikāyai namaḥ

Salutations to Her who is the original Mantra (Mūla-mantra, here Pañca daś'ākṣarī) itself.

89. ओं मूलकूटत्रय - कलेबरायै नमः

Om mūla - kūṭa - traya - kalebarāyai namaḥ

Salutations to Her whose body is identical with Pañca - daś'ākṣarī Mantra with all its Kūṭas or combination of letters.

90. ओं कुलामृतैक - रसिकायै नमः

Om kul'āmṛt'aika - rasikāyai namaḥ

Salutations to Her who (as the Kundalinī) revels in the nectar flowing from the Sahasrāra through the whole of the Kula path (i.e. the Suṣumnā).

91. ओं कुलसंकेत-पालिन्यै नमः

Om kula-saṅketa-pālinyai namah

Salutations to Her who guards the esoteric doctrine of the Kaulas.

92. ओं कुलांगनायै नमः

Om kul'āṅganāyai namaḥ

Salutations to Her who is the Female Element (Kundalinī) in the Kula Path.

93. ओं कुलान्तस्थायै नमः

Om kul'āntasthāyai namaḥ

Salutations to Her who is the innermost Reality of the Kula Path.

94. ओं कौलिन्यै नमः

Om kaulinyai namah

Salutations to Her who is called Kaulinī, the core of the Kaula form of worship.

95. ओं कुलयोगिन्यै नमः

Om kula-yoginyai namaḥ

Salutations to Her who is the Deity of the Kaulas.

96. ओं अकुलायै नमः

Om akulāyai namaḥ

Salutations to Her who is also the Akula (Siva) who is in the thousand-petalled lotus above the Kula Path.

97. ओं समयान्तस्थायै नमः

Om samay'āntasthāyai namah

Salutations to Her who is likewise the centre of the Samaya doctrine (in which the worship is done internally through meditation and which holds Śiva-Śakti as of equal importance in all respects).

98. ओं समयाचार-तत्परायै नमः

Om samay'ācāra-tatparāyai namaḥ

Salutations to Her to whom the Samaya tradition of worship is dear.

99. ओं मूलाधारैक-निलयायै नमः

Om mul'ādhār'aika-nilāyayai namah

Salutations to Her whose chief residence is the Mul'ādhāra.

100. ओं ब्रह्मग्रन्थि-विभेदिन्यै नमः

Om brahma-granthi-vibhedinyai namaḥ

Salutations to Her who in Her ascent from the Mul'ādhāra breaks through the Brahma-granthi (the Barrier of Brahmā to the subtle dimension).

101. ओं मणिपूरान्तरुदितायै नमः

Om maṇipūr'āntar - uditāyai namaḥ

Salutations to Her who then emerges in the Maṇipūra - cakra.

102. ओं विष्णुग्रन्थि - विभेदिन्यै नमः

Om viṣṇu - granthi - vibhedinyai namaḥ

Salutations to Her who then breaks through the Viṣṇu - granthi (the barrier to still subtler dimensions).

103. ओं आज्ञाचक्रान्तरालस्थायै नमः

Om ājñā - cakr'āntarālasthāyai namaḥ

Salutations to Her who next abides in the centre of the Ājñā - cakra.

104. ओं रुद्रग्रन्थि - विभेदिन्यै नमः

Om rudra - granthi - vibhedinyai namaḥ

Salutations to Her who finally breaks through the Rudra - granthi (the barrier to the subtlest dimension).

105. ओं सहस्त्रारांबुजारूढायै नमः

Om sahasrār'āmbuj'ārūḍhāyai namaḥ

Salutations to Her who then ascends to the Thousand - petalled Lotus known as the Sahasrāra.

106. ओं सुधासाराभिवर्षिण्यै नमः

Om sudhā - sār'ābhivarṣiṇyai namaḥ

Salutations to Her who sends streams of Nectar (spiritual bliss) from the Transcendant moon in the Sahasrāra.

107. ओं तडिल्लता - समरुच्यै नमः

Om tadil - latā - sama - rucyai namaḥ

Salutations to Her who shines like a steady flash of lightning.

108. ओं षट्चक्रोपरि - संस्थितायै नमः

Om ṣaṭ - cakr'opari - samsthitāyai namaḥ

Salutations to Her who then establishes herself above the six Cakras.

109. ओं महासक्त्यै नमः

Om mah'āsaktyai namaḥ

Salutations to Her whose immense joy consists in Āsakti (union with śiva).

110. ओं कुण्डलिन्यै नमः

Om kuṇḍalinyai namaḥ

Salutations to Her who resides in the Mūlādhāra as the Kuṇḍalinī (the coiled power).

111. ओं बिसतन्तु - तनीयस्यै नमः

Om bisa - tantu - tanīyasyai namaḥ

Salutations to Her who is as fine and firm as the fibre of a lotus stalk.

112. ओं भवान्यै नमः

Om bhavānyai namaḥ

Salutations to Her who is Bhavānī, the consort of Bhava (Śiva).

113. ओं भावनागम्यायै नमः

Om bhāvanā - gamyāyai namaḥ

Salutations to Her who is realised through devoted meditation.

114. ओं भवारण्य - कुठारिकायै नमः

Om bhav'āraṇya- kuṭhārikāyai namaḥ

Salutations to Her who is verily like an axe for clearing the jungle of Samsāra (transmigratory existence) in which the Jīva is caught.

115. ओं भद्रप्रियायै नमः

Om bhadra - priyāyai namaḥ

Salutations to Her who is fond of everything auspicious.

116. ओं भद्रमूर्तये नमः

Om bhadra - mūrtaye namaḥ

Salutations to Her who is the embodiment of auspiciousness.

117. ओं भक्त - सौभाग्य - दायिन्यै नमः

Om bhakta - saubhāgya - dāyinyai namaḥ

Salutations to Her who grants all - round advancement to devotees, both in the spiritual and the material fields.

118. ओं भक्तिप्रियायै नमः

Om bhakti - priyāyai namaḥ

Salutations to Her who is fond of true devotion.

119. ओं भक्तिगम्यायै नमः

Om bhakti - gamyāyai namaḥ

Salutations to Her who is attained through true devotion.

120. ओं भक्तिवश्यायै नमः

Om bhakti - vaśyāyai namaḥ

Salutations to Her who can be won over through true devotion.

121. ओं भयापहायै नमः

Om bhay'āpahāyai namaḥ

Salutations to Her who dispels all fear.

122. ओं शांभव्यै नमः

Om śāmbhavyai namaḥ

Salutations to Her who is known as Śāmbhavī, the Consort of Śiva.

123. ओं शारदाराध्यायै नमः

Om śārad'ārādhyāyai namaḥ

Salutations to Her who is adored by Sāradā (the Consort of Brahma).

124. ओं शर्वाण्यै नमः

Om śarvāṇyai namaḥ

Salutations to Her who is the consort of Śarva or Śiva.

125. ओं शर्मदायिन्यै नमः

Om śarmadāyinyai namaḥ

Salutations to Her who is the bestower of happiness.

126. ओं शांकर्यै नमः

Om śāṅkaryai namaḥ

Salutations to Her who is Śaṅkarī the consort of Śiva, who is inseparable from Her.

127. ओं श्रीकर्यै नमः

Om śrīkaryai namaḥ

Salutations to Her who is the spouse of Viṣṇu, who brings prosperity to devotees.

128. ओं साध्व्यै नमः

Om sādhvyai namaḥ

Salutations to Her who is a paragon of virtue.

129. ओं शरच्चन्द्र - निभाननायै नमः

Om śarac - candra - nibh'ānanā'yai namaḥ

Salutations to Her whose face shines like the autumnal moon.

130. ओं शातोदर्यै नमः

Om śāt'odaryai namaḥ

Salutations to Her who has a very slender waist.

131. ओं शान्तिमत्यै नमः

Om śāntimatyai namaḥ

Salutations to Her who is full of peace.

132. ओं निराधारायै नमः

Om nirādhārāyai namaḥ

Salutations to Her who has no support other than Herself, but supports everything else.

133. ओं निरंजनायै नमः

Oṃ nirañjanāyai namaḥ

Salutations to Her who is free from the stain of Ignorance.

134. ओं निर्लेपायै नमः

Om nirlepāyai namaḥ

Salutations to Her who is free from all affectations of external contacts.

135. ओं निर्मलायै नमः

Om nirmalāyai namaḥ

Salutations to Her who is free from all impurities.

136. ओं नित्यायै नमः

Om niṭyāyai namaḥ

Salutations to Her who is eternal.

137. ओं निराकारायै नमः

Om nirākārāyai namaḥ

Salutations to Her who is not limited to and by any form.

138. ओं निराकुलायै नमः

Om nirākulāyai namaḥ

Salutations to Her who is never agitated.

139. ओं निर्गुणायै नमः

Om nirguṇāyai namaḥ

Salutations to Her who is beyond the three Guṇas of Prakrti - Sattva, Rajas and Tamas.

140. ओं निष्कलायै नमः

Om niṣkalāyai namaḥ

Salutations to Her who is the Partless Unitary Whole.

141. ओं शान्तायै नमः

Om śāntāyai namaḥ

Salutations to Her who is ever serene.

142. ओं निष्कामायै नमः

Om niṣkāmāyai namaḥ

Salutations to Her who is free from desires.

143. ओं निरुपप्लवायै नमः

Om nir - upaplavāyai namaḥ

Salutations to Her who is free from afflictions.

144. ओं नित्यमुक्तायै नमः

Om nitya - muktāyai namaḥ

Salutations to Her who is eternally free.

145. ओं निर्विकारायै नमः

Om nirvikārāyai namaḥ

Salutations to Her who is not subject to change.

146. ओं निष्प्रपंचायै नमः

Om niṣprapañcāyai namaḥ

Salutations to Her who is beyond the sphere of multiplicity.

147. ओं निराश्रयायै नमः

Om nirāśrayāyai namaḥ

Salutations to Her who is not dependent on anything or anyone.

148. ओं नित्यशुद्धायै नमः

Om nitya - śuddhāyai namaḥ

Salutations to Her who is eternally pure.

149. ओं नित्यबुद्धायै नमः

Om nitya - buddhāyai namaḥ

Salutations to Her who is the ever - awake Consciousness.

150. ओं निरवद्यायै नमः

Om nir - avadyāyai namaḥ

Salutations to Her who is flawless.

151. ओं निरन्तरायै नमः

Om nir - antarāyai namaḥ

Salutations to Her who is without any division, being eternal by nature.

152. ओं निष्कारणायै नमः

Om niṣ - kāraṇāyai namaḥ

Salutations to Her who has no cause for Herself, as she is the first cause.

153. ओं निष्कलंकायै नमः

Om niṣ - kalaṅkāyai namaḥ

Salutations to Her who is without any stain.

154. ओं निरुपाधये नमः

Om nir - upādhaye namaḥ

Salutations to Her who has no limitations.

155. ओं निरीश्वरायै नमः

Om nir - īśvarāyai namaḥ

Salutations to Her who has no over - lord.

156. ओं नीरागायै नमः

Om nīrāgāyai namaḥ

Salutations to Her who is without passions.

157. ओं रागमथन्यै नमः

Om rāga - mathanyai namaḥ

Salutations to Her who destroys all passion in the minds of devotees.

158. ओं निर्मदायै नमः

Om nir - madāyai namaḥ

Salutations to Her who is without pride.

159. ओं मदनाशिन्यै नमः

Om mada - nāśinyai namaḥ

Salutations to Her who destroys all pride.

160. ओं निश्चिन्तायै नमः

Om niścintāyai namaḥ

Salutations to Her who is free from all doubts and anxieties.

161. ओं निरहंकारायै नमः

Om nir - ahaṅkārāyai namah

Salutations to Her who is without any egoism.

162. ओं निर्मोहायै नमः

Om nir - mohāyai namaḥ

Salutations to Her who is free from false view of things.

163. ओं मोहनाशिन्यै नमः

Om moha - nāśinyai namaḥ

Salutations to Her who dispels all illusions.

164. ओं निर्ममायै नमः

Om nir - mamāyai namaḥ

Salutations to Her who is devoid of self

interest in any matter, as She includes everything in Herself.

165. ओं ममताहन्त्र्यै नमः

Om mamatā - hantryai namaḥ

Salutations to Her who destroys the sense of self - centredness in devotees.

166. ओं निष्पापायै नमः

Om niṣpāpāyai namaḥ

Salutations to Her who is sinless.

167. ओं पापनाशिन्यै नमः

Om pāpa - nāśinyai namaḥ

Salutations to Her who destroys sins together with the root of all sinful tendencies.

168. निष्क्रोधायै नमः

Om niṣkrodhāyai namaḥ

Salutations to Her who is without anger.

169. ओं क्रोधशमन्यै नमः

Om krodha - śamanyai namaḥ

Salutations to Her who destroys the tendency to get angry.

170. ओं निर्लोभायै नमः

Om nirlobhāyai namaḥ

Salutations to Her who is free from greed.

171. ओं लोभनाशिन्यै नमः

Om lobha - nāśinyai namaḥ

Salutations to Her who destroys greed in Her devotees.

172. ओं निःसंशयायै नमः

Om niḥsamśayāyai namaḥ

Salutations to Her who has no doubts.

173. ओं संशयघ्न्यै नमः

Om samśayaghnyai namaḥ

Salutations to Her who effaces all doubts.

174. ओं निर्भवायै नमः

Om nir - bhavāyai namaḥ

Salutations to Her who is not involved in the cycle of births and deaths.

175. ओं भवनाशिन्यै नमः

Om bhava - nāśinyai namaḥ

Salutations to Her who frees devotees from involvement in the cycle of births and deaths.

176. ओं निर्विकल्पायै नमः

Om nir - vikalpāyai namaḥ

Salutations to Her who is without any modifications, as she is pure consciousness.

177. ओं निराबाधायै नमः

Om nir'ābādhāyai namaḥ

Salutations to Her who can never be sublated.

178. ओं निर्भेदायै नमः

Om nir - bhedāyai namaḥ

Salutations to Her who is beyond all differences.

179. ओं भेदनाशिन्यै नमः

Om bheda - nāśinyai namaḥ

Salutations to Her who destroys the sense of differences.

180. ओं निर्नाशायै नमः

Om nirnāśāyai namaḥ

Salutations to Her who is deathless.

181. ओं मृत्युमथन्यै नमः

Om mṛtyu - mathanyai namaḥ

Salutations to Her who destroys the fear of death.

182. ओं निष्क्रियायै नमः

Om niṣkriyāyai namaḥ

Salutations to Her who is without involvement in action.

183. ओं निष्परिग्रहायै नमः

Om niṣparigrahāyai namaḥ

Salutations to Her who needs no gift, as everything in the universe is hers.

184. ओं निस्तुलायै नमः

Om nistulāyai namaḥ

Salutations to Her who is peerless.

185. ओं नीलचिकुरायै नमः

Om nīla - cikurāyai namaḥ

Salutations to Her whose locks of hair are shining black in colour.

186. ओं निरपायायै नमः

Om nir - apāyāyai namaḥ

Salutations to Her who is imperishable.

187. ओं निरत्ययायै नमः

Om niratyayāyai namaḥ

Salutations to Her who is indestructible.

188. ओं दुर्लभायै नमः

Om durlabhāyai namaḥ

Salutations to Her who is difficult to attain.

189. ओं दुर्गमायै नमः

Om durgamāyai namaḥ

Salutations to Her who is hard to approach.

190. ओं दुर्गायै नमः

Om durgāyai namaḥ

Salutations to Her who is difficult of access.

191. ओं दुःखहन्त्र्यै नमः

Om duḥkha - hantryai namaḥ

Salutations to Her who puts an end to sorrow.

192. ओं सुखप्रदायै नमः

Om sukha - pradāyai namaḥ

Salutations to Her who bestows all happiness.

193. ओं दुष्टदूरायै नमः

Om duṣṭa - dūrāyai namaḥ

Salutations to Her who is far away for the wicked.

194. ओं दुराचारशमन्यै नमः

Om dur'ācāra - śamanyai namaḥ

Salutations to Her who puts an end to evil ways.

195. ओं दोष - वर्जितायै नमः

Om doṣa - varjitāyai namaḥ

Salutations to Her who is free from all evil.

196. ओं सर्वज्ञायै नमः

Om sarvajñāyai namaḥ

Salutations to Her who is omniscient.

197. ओं सान्द्रकरुणायै नमः

Om sāndra - karuṇāyai namaḥ

Salutations to Her who is deeply compassionate.

198. ओं समानाधिक - वर्जितायै नमः

Om samān'ādhika - varjitāyai namaḥ

Salutations to Her who has none equal or superior.

199. ओं सर्वशक्तिमय्यै नमः

Om sarva - śakti - mayyai namaḥ

Salutations to Her to whom the powers associated with all deities belong.

200. ओं सर्वमंगलायै नमः

Om sarva - maṅgalāyai namaḥ

Salutations to Her who is all auspiciousness.

201. ओं सद्गति - प्रदायै नमः

Om sad - gati - pradāyai namaḥ

Salutations to Her who leads one along the path of salvation.

202. ओं सर्वेश्वर्यै नमः

Om sarv'eśvaryai namaḥ

Salutations to Her who is the Mistress of the whole universe.

203. ओं सर्वमय्यै नमः

Om sarva - mayyai namaḥ

Salutations to Her who is the all.

204. ओं सर्वमन्त्र - स्वरूपिण्यै नमः

Om sarva - mantra - svarūpiṇyai namaḥ

Salutations to Her who is the essence of all Mantras.

205. ओं सर्व - यन्त्रात्मिकायै नमः

Om sarva - yantr'ātmikāyai namaḥ

Salutations to Her who is the soul of all Yantras (mystic diagrams).

206. ओं सर्व - तन्त्ररूपायै नमः

Om sarva - tantra - rūpāyai namaḥ

Salutations to Her who is the embodiment of all Tantras (scriptures dealing with worship).

207. ओं मनोन्मन्यै नमः

Om man'onmanyai namaḥ

Salutations to Her who is Manonmanī, the transcendent consciouness.

208. ओं माहेश्वर्यै नमः

Om māh'eśvaryai namaḥ

Salutations to Her who is the Consort of Maheśvara, the Supreme Ruler of the Universe.

209. ओं महादेव्यै नमः

Om mahā - devyai namaḥ

Salutations to Her who is the Supreme Goddess.

210. ओं महालक्ष्म्यै नमः

Om mahā - lakṣmyai namaḥ

Salutations to Her who is Mahālakṣmī.

211. ओं मृडप्रियायै नमः

Om mṛḍa - priyāyai namaḥ

Salutations to Her who is the beloved of Mṛḍa (Śiva).

212. ओं महारूपायै नमः

Om mahā - rūpāyai namaḥ

Salutations to Her whose form is magnificent and all - embracing.

213. ओं महापूज्यायै नमः

Om mahā - pūjyāyai namaḥ

Salutations to Her who is the most worshipful.

214. ओं महा - पातक - नाशिन्यै नमः

Om mahā - pātaka - nāśinyai namaḥ

Salutations to Her who can destroy the effects of even the most heinous sins.

215. ओं महामायायै नमः

Om mahā - māyāyai namaḥ

Salutations to Her who is Mahāmāyā (Supreme Power).

216. ओं महासत्त्वायै नमः

Om mahā - sattvāyai namaḥ

Salutations to Her who is the Supreme Reality (Sattva).

217. ओं महाशक्त्यै नमः

Om mahā - śaktyai namaḥ

Salutations to Her who is the Boundless Energy.

218. ओं महारत्यै नमः

Om mahā - ratyai namaḥ

Salutations to Her who is boundless delight.

219. ओं महाभोगायै नमः

Om mahā - bhogāyai namaḥ

Salutations to Her who is the great enjoyer.

220. ओं महैश्वर्यायै नमः

Om mah'aiśvaryāyai namaḥ

Salutations to Her who possesses supreme lordliness.

221. ओं महावीर्यायै नमः

Om mahā - vīryāyai namaḥ

Salutations to Her who is supreme in valour.

222. ओं महाबलायै नमः

Om mahā - balāyai namah

Salutations to Her who is supreme in strength.

223. ओं महाबुद्ध्यै नमः

Om mahā - buddhyai namaḥ

Salutations to Her who is supreme in wisdom.

224. ओं महासिद्ध्यै नमः

Om mahā - siddhyai namaḥ

Salutations to Her who is endowed with the highest of attainments (siddhi).

225. ओं महायोगेश्वरेश्वर्यै नमः

Om mahā - yogeśvar'eśvaryai namaḥ

Salutations to Her who is the object of worship for all Yogeśvaras (spiritual adepts).

226. ओं महातन्त्रायै नमः

Om mahā - tantrāyai namaḥ

Salutations to Her who is Herself the greatest Tantra.

227. ओं महामन्त्रायै नमः

Om mahā - mantrāyai namaḥ

Salutations to Her who is the greatest Mantra (Srī Vidyā).

228. ओं महायन्त्रायै नमः

Om mahā - yantrāyai namaḥ

Salutations to Her who is the greatest Yantra (Śrīyantra or Śrīcakra).

229. ओं महासनायै नमः

Om mah'āsanāyai namaḥ

Salutations to Her who is seated on the great seat (the thirty six Tattvas).

230. ओं महायाग - क्रमाराध्यायै नमः

Om mahā - yāga - kram'ārādhyāyai namaḥ

Salutations to Her who is adored by Mahā - yāga (supreme Sacrifice).

231. ओं महाभैरव - पूजितायै नमः

Om mahā - bhairava - pūjitāyai namaḥ

Salutations to Her who is worshipped by Mahābhairavā (Śiva)

232. ओं महेश्वर - महाकल्प - महाताण्डव - साक्षिण्यै नमः

Om mah'eśvara - mahā - kalpa mahā'tāṇḍava sākṣiṇyai namaḥ

Salutations to Her who is the witness of the Supreme Lord's (Mah'eśvara's) awesome destructive cosmic dance at the end of the creative cycle.

233. ओं महाकामेश - महिष्यै नमः

Om mahā - kāmeśa - mahiṣyai namaḥ

Salutations to Her who is the consort of the great Lord of desire (Mahā - kāmeśa).

234. ओं महात्रिपुरसुन्दर्यै नमः

Om mahā - tripura - sundaryai namaḥ

Salutations to Her who is Tripura - sundarī (the Divine Beauty known by that name).

235. ओं चतुष्षष्ट्युपचाराढ्यायै नमः

Om catuḥ - ṣaṣṭ'yupacār'āḍhyāyai namaḥ

Salutations to Her who is worshipped with sixty four ingredients (Upacāras).

236. ओं चतुष्षष्टिकलामय्यै नमः

Om catuḥ - ṣaṣti - kalā - mayyai namaḥ

Salutations to Her who embodies the sixty - four forms of fine arts.

237. ओं महाचतुः - षष्टिकोटि - योगिनी - गणसेवितायै नमः

Om mahā - catuḥ - ṣaṣti - koṭi - yoginī - gaṇa - sevitāyai namaḥ

Salutations to Her who is attended on by a host of sixty - four crores of Yoginis.

238. ओं मनुविद्यायै नमः

Om manu - vidyāyai namaḥ

Salutations to Her who is the subject of Manuvidyā (Śrīvidyā having twelve traditional authorities headed by Manu).

239. ओं चन्द्रविद्यायै नमः

Om candra - vidyāyai namaḥ

Salutations to Her who is the subject of Candravidyā (the same Śrīvidyā as practised by Chandra, one of the twelve authorities).

240. ओं चन्द्रमण्डल - मध्यगायै नमः

Om candra - maṇḍala - madhyagāyai namaḥ

Salutations to Her who is stationed in the centre of the moon (the pericap of the Sahasrāra).

241. ओं चारुरूपायै नमः

Om cāru - rūpayai namaḥ

Salutations to Her whose form is exquisite.

242. ओं चारुहासायै नमः

Om cāru - hāsāyai namaḥ

Salutations to Her whose smile is charming.

243. ओं चारुचन्द्र - कलाधरायै नमः

Om cāru - candra - kalā - dharāyai namaḥ.

Salutations to Her who has the comely crescent moon in Her crown.

244. ओं चराचर - जगन्नाथायै नमः

Om car'ācara - jagan - nāṭhāyai namaḥ

Salutations to Her who is the queen ruling over all beings sentient and insentient.

245. ओं चक्रराज - निकेतनायै नमः

Om cakra - rāja - niketanāyai namaḥ

Salutations to Her who has Her abode in Cakra - rāja or Śrīcakra.

246. ओं पार्वत्यै नमः

Om pārvatyai namaḥ

Salutations to Her who is Pārvatī, the daughter of the Himālayas.

247. ओं पद्मनयनायै नमः

Om padma - nayanāyai namaḥ

Salutations to Her whose eyes are like a lotus petal.

248. ओं पद्मराग - समप्रभायै नमः

Om padma - rāga - sama - prabhāyai namaḥ

Salutations to Her who shines like a ruby.

249. ओं पंचप्रेतासनासीनायै नमः

Om pañca - pretāsan'āsīnāyai namaḥ

Salutations to Her who sits on a seat formed of the five dead deities (same as the Brahmas mentioned below).

250. ओं पंचब्रह्मस्वरूपिण्यै नमः

Om pañca - brahma - svarūpiṇyai namaḥ

Salutations to Her whose form is composed of five Brahmas (Brahmā, Viṣṇu, Rudra, Īśvara and Sadāśiva).

251. ओं चिन्मय्यै नमः

Om cinmayyai namaḥ

Salutations to Her who is Pure Consciousness.

252. ओं परमानन्दायै नमः

Om param'ānandāyai namaḥ

Salutations to Her who is Supreme Bliss.

253. ओं विज्ञानघनरूपिण्यै नमः

Om vijñāna - ghana - rūpiṇyai namaḥ

Salutations to Her who is wisdom crystallized.

254. ओं ध्यान - ध्यातृ - ध्येयरूपायै नमः

Om dhyāna - dhyātṛ - dhyeya - rūpāyai namaḥ

Salutations to Her who is meditation, the person meditating and the object meditated upon.

255. ओं धर्माधर्म - विवर्जितायै नमः

Om dharm'ādharma - vivarjitāyai namaḥ

Salutations to Her who transcends both good and evil.

256. ओं विश्वरूपायै नमः

Om viśva - rūpāyai namaḥ

Salutations to Her who has the whole world perceived in the waking state as Her form, and who is therefore technically called Viśva.

257. ओं जागरिण्यै नमः

Om jāgariṇyai namaḥ

Salutations to Her who is the waking state.

258. ओं स्वपन्त्यै नमः

Om svapantyai namaḥ

Salutations to Her who is the Dream State.

259. ओं तैजसात्मिकायै नमः

Om taijas'ātmikāyai namaḥ

Salutations to Her who is the soul of Taijasā, the totality of Jīvas experiencing the Dream State.

260. ओं सुप्तायै नमः

Om suptāyai namaḥ

Salutations to Her who is the state of Deep Sleep.

261. ओं प्राज्ञात्मिकायै नमः

Om prājñ'ātmikāyai namaḥ

Salutations to Her who is the soul of the totality of Jīvas experiencing Deep Sleep.

262. ओं तुर्यायै नमः

Om turyāyai namaḥ

Salutations to Her who is the Turīya which transcends all states.

263. ओं सर्वावस्था - विवर्जितायै नमः

Om sarv'āvasthā - vivarjitāyai namaḥ

Salutations to Her who is devoid of all states.

264. ओं सृष्टिकर्त्र्यै नमः

Om sṛṣṭi - kartryai namaḥ

Salutations to Her who is the cause of creation.

265. ओं ब्रह्मरूपायै नमः

Om brahma - rūpāyai namaḥ

Salutations to Her who has taken the form of Brahmā for creation.

266. ओं गोप्त्र्यै नमः

Om goptryai namaḥ

Salutations to Her whose function is protection.

267. ओं गोविन्दरूपिण्यै नमः

Om govinda - rūpiṇyai namaḥ

Salutations to Her who has taken the form of Govinda (Viṣṇu) for this purpose.

268. ओं संहारिण्यै नमः

Om samhāriṇyai namaḥ

Salutations to Her whose function is to destroy the universe.

269. ओं रुद्ररूपायै नमः

Om rudra - rūpāyai namaḥ

Salutations to Her who takes the form of Rudra for this purpose.

270. ओं तिरोधानकर्यै नमः

Om tirodhāna - karyai namaḥ

Salutations to Her whose function is concealing this,i.e. reducing this universe to its primeval conditions.

271. ओं ईश्वर्यै नमः

Om īśvaryai namaḥ

Salutations to Her who is Īśvarī who accomplishes this.

272. ओं सदाशिवायै नमः

Om sadā - śivāyai namaḥ

Salutations to Her who is Sadāśivā.

273. ओं अनुग्रहदायै नमः

Om anugraha - dāyai namaḥ

Salutations to Her who by Her gracious blessing starts the universe again on the path of evolution from the involved state.

274. ओं पंचकृत्यपरायणायै नमः

Om pañca - kṛtya - parāyaṇāyai namaḥ

Salutations to Her who is engaged in the five functions mentioned above.

275. ओं भानुमण्डल - मध्यस्थायै नमः

Om bhānu - maṇḍala - madhyasthāyai namaḥ

Salutations to Her who is meditated upon as stationed in the centre of the solar orb.

276. ओं भैरव्यै नमः

Om bhairavyai namaḥ

Salutations to Her who is Bhairavī, the terror - generating Deity.

277. ओं भगमालिन्यै नमः

Om bhaga - mālinyai namaḥ

Salutations to Her who is Bhaga-mālinī — the Mother having the six Bhagas or excellences (lordliness, righteousness, glory, beauty, omniscience and detachment).

278. ओं पद्मासनायै नमः

Om pad'māsanāyai naṁaḥ

Salatations to Her who is Brahmā, with seat in the cosmic lotus.

279. ओं भगवत्यै नमः

Om bhagavatyai namaḥ

Salutations to Her who is the Bhagavatī or the supreme goddess.

280. ओं पद्मनाभ - सहोदर्यै नमः

Om padma - nābha - sahodaryai namaḥ

Salutations to Her who is the sister of Padmanābha or Mahāviṣṇu.

281. ओं उन्मेष-निमिषोत्पन्न-विपन्न-भुवनावल्यै नमः

Om unmeṣa-nimiṣ'otpanna-vipanna-bhuvan'āvalyai namaḥ

Salutations to Her the opening of whose eyes results in creation and closing in destuction.

282. ओं सहस्रशीर्षवदनायै नमः

Om sahasra-śīrṣa-vadanāyai namaḥ

Salutations to Her who has thousands of heads and faces.

283. ओं सहस्राक्ष्यै नमः

Om sahasr'ākṣyai namaḥ

Salutations to Her who has thousands of eyes.

284. ओं सहस्रपदे नमः

Om sahasra-pade namaḥ

Salutations to Her who has thousands of feet.

285. ओं आब्रह्म-कीट-जनन्यै नमः

Om ābrahma-kīṭa-jananyai namaḥ

Salutations to the generator of all from Brahmā down to a worm.

286. ओं वर्णाश्रम-विधायिन्यै नमः

Om varṇ'āśrama-vidhāyinyai namaḥ

Salutations to Her who ordained the social divisions and stations in life.

287. ओं निजाज्ञारूप-निगमायै नमः

Om nij'ājña-rūpa-nigamāyai namaḥ

Salutations to Her whose commands the Vedas are.

288. ओं पुण्यापुण्य-फलप्रदायै नमः

Om puṇy'āpuṇya-phala-pradāyai namaḥ

Salutations to Her who is the dispenser of the fruits of righteous as also of evil actions.

289. ओं श्रुति-सीमन्त-सिन्दूरी-कृत-पादाब्जधूलिकायै नमः

Om śruti-sīmanta-sindurī-kṛta-pād'ābja-dhūlikāyai namaḥ

Salutations to Her the dust of whose feet are borne on their head by the Śruti Devatas (Vedas personified as goddesses), who prostrate before Her and thereby colour Her feet with the vermilion marks on their foreheads.

290. ओं सकलागम-संदोह-शुक्ति-संपुट-मौक्तिकायै नमः

Om sakal'āgama-sandoha-śukti-samputa-mauktikāyai namaḥ

Salutations to Her who is the priceless pearl contained in the shell casket of all the Āgamas (ritualistic scriptures).

291. ओं पुरुषार्थ-प्रदायै नमः

Om puruṣ'ārtha-pradāyai-namaḥ

Salutations to Her who bestows the fourfold values of human life —Dharma (morality), Artha (wealth), Kāma (pleasure) and Moksa (liberation).

292. ओं पूर्णायै नमः

Om pūrṇāyai namaḥ

Salutations to Her who is Pūrṇa (the all-encompassing whole).

293. ओं भोगिन्यै नमः

Om bhoginyai namaḥ

Salutations to Her who is ever full of bliss.

294. ओं भुवनेश्वर्यै नमः

Om bhuvan'eśvaryai namaḥ

Salutations to Her who is Bhuvan'eśvarī, the sovereign of the universe.

295. ओं अंबिकायै नमः

Om ambikāyai namaḥ

Salutations to Her who is Ambikā, the Mother of the Universe, possessing of the powers known as Icchā (will), Jñāna (cognition) and Kriyā (action).

296. ओं अनादि-निधनायै नमः

Om anādi-nidhanāyai namaḥ

Salutations to Her who exists without a beginning or an end.

297. ओं हरिब्रह्मेन्द्र-सेवितायै नमः

Om hari-brahm'endra-sevitāyai namaḥ

Salutations to Her who is adored even by Deities like Hari, Brahmā and Indra.

298. ओं नारायण्यै नमः

Om nārāyaṇyai namaḥ

Salutations to Her who is Nārāyanī, the counterpart of Nārāyaṇa (Viṣṇu).

299. ओं नादरूपायै नमः

Om nāda-rūpāyai namaḥ

Salutations to Her who is in the form of Nāda (cosmic sound).

300. ओं नामरूप-विवर्जितायै नमः

Om nāma-rūpa-vivarjitāyai namaḥ

Salutations to Her who as Para-Brahman is without name and form.

301. ओं ह्रींकार्यै नमः

Om hrīṅ-kāryai namaḥ

Salutations to Her who is seed-syllable (Bījā'kṣara) Hrīm, which represents Bhuvan'esvarī who creates, sustains and dissolves the universe.

302. ओं ह्रीमत्यै नमः

Om hrīmatyai namaḥ

Salutations to Her who is endowed with modesty.

303. ओं हृद्यायै नमः

Om hṛdyāyai namaḥ

Salutations to Her who dwells in the heart and thereby gives highest satisfaction.

304. ओं हेयोपादेय-वर्जितायै नमः

Om hey'opādeya-varjitāyai namaḥ

Salutations to Her who has nothing to reject nor to seek.

305. ओं राजराजार्चितायै नमः

Om rāja-rāj'ārcitāyai namaḥ

Salutations to Her who is Kubera, the lord of wealth, described as the kings of kings. or worshipped by Kubera, the king of kings.

306. ओं राज्ञ्यै नमः

Om rājñyai namaḥ

Salutations to Her who is the queen (Śakti) of the Supreme Being.

307. ओं रम्यायै नमः

Om ramyāyai namaḥ

Salutations to Her who is lovely.

308. ओं राजीव-लोचनायै नमः

Om rājīva-locanāyai namah

Salutations to Her whose eyes are lotus-like.

309. ओं रञ्जन्यै नमः

Om rañjanyai namaḥ

Salutations to Her who gives delight.

310. ओं रमण्यै नमः

Om ramaṇyai namaḥ

Salutations to Her who is charming.

311. ओं रस्यायै नमः

Om rasyāyai namah

Salutations to Her who is the essence of all things we enjoy.

312. ओं रणत्किंकिणि-मेखलायै नमः

Om raṇat-kiṅkiṇi-mekhalāyai namaḥ

Salutations to Her who wears a girdle of tinkling bells.

313. ओं रमायै नमः

Om ramāyai namaḥ

Salutations to Her who is Ramā(Lakṣmī).

314. ओं राकेन्दु-वदनायै नमः

Om rākendu-vadanāyai namaḥ

Salutations to Her whose face is like the full moon.

315. ओं रतिरूपायै नमः

Om rati-rūpāyai namaḥ

Salutations to Her whose form is like that of Rati, the wife of Kāmadeva (god of love).

316. ओं रतिप्रियायै नमः

Om rati-priyāyai namaḥ

Salutations to Her who is dear to Rati.

317. ओं रक्षाकर्यै नमः

Om rakṣā-karyai namaḥ

Salutations to Her who is saviour of Jīvas from Samsāra.

318. ओं राक्षसघ्न्यै नमः

Om rākṣasa-ghnyai namaḥ

Salutations to Her who is the slayer of Rākṣasas, the forces of evil.

319. ओं रामायै नमः

Om rāmāyai namaḥ

Salutations to Her who is all that is feminine.

320. ओं रमणलंपटायै नमः

Om ramaṇa-lampaṭāyai namaḥ

Salutations to Her who craves to sport with Her Consort.

321. ओं काम्यायै नमः

Om kāmyāyai namaḥ

Salutations to Her who is to be longed for as the highest.

322. ओं कामकलारूपायै नमः

Om kāma-kalā-rūpāyai namaḥ

Salutations to Her who is Kāma-kalā, the manifestation of Kāmeśvara and Kāmeśvari together.

323. ओं कदंब-कुसुम-प्रियायै नमः

Om kadamba-kusuma-priyāyai namaḥ

Salutations to Her who is fond of Kadamba flowers.

324. ओं कल्याण्यै नमः

Om kalyāṇyai namaḥ

Salutations to Her who is Kalyāṇī or the Blessed One.

325. ओं जगती-कन्दायै नमः

Om jagatī-kandāyai namaḥ

Salutations to Her who is the Root of the Universe.

326. ओं करुणा-रस-सागरायै नमः

Om karuṇā-rasa-sāgarāyai namaḥ

Salutations to Her who is the sea of compassion.

327. ओं कलावत्यै नमः

Om kalāvatyai namaḥ

Salutations to Her who is the embodiment of all arts.

328. ओं कलालापायै नमः

Om kal'ālāpāyai namaḥ

Salutations to Her whose speech itself constitutes what is called fine art.

329. ओं कान्तायै नमः

Om kāntāyai namaḥ

Salutations to Her who is Beauty coveted by all.

330. ओं कादंबरी-प्रियायै नमः

Om kādambarī-priyāyai namaḥ

Salutations to Her who is fond of offerings of Kādambarī (mead).

331. ओं वरदायै नमः

Om varadāyai namaḥ

Salutations to Her who bestows boons.

332. ओं वामनयनायै नमः

Om vāma-nayanāyai namaḥ

Salutations to Her whose eyes are full of grace.

333. ओं वारुणी-मद-विह्वलायै नमः

Om vāruṇī-mada-vihvalāyai namaḥ

Salutations to Her who is intoxicated with Vāruṇī (the wine of spiritual bliss).

334. ओं विश्वाधिकायै नमः

Om viśv'ādhikāyai namaḥ

Salutations to Her who transcends the whole universe.

335. ओं वेदवेद्यायै नमः

Om veda-vedyāyai namaḥ

Salutations to Her who can be known through the Vedas (Sacred scriptures).

336. ओं विन्ध्याचल-निवासिन्यै नमः

Om vindhy'ācala-nivāsinyai namaḥ

Salutations to Her whose abode is in the Vindhyā Mountain.

337. ओं विधात्र्यै नमः

Om vidhātryai namaḥ

Salutations to Her who created the universe and sustains it.

338. ओं वेदजनन्यै नमः

Om veda-jananyai namaḥ

Salutations to Her who is the source of the world.

339. ओं विष्णुमायायै नमः

Om viṣṇu-māyāyai namaḥ

Salutations to Her who is Viṣṇu-māya—the power that limits the all-pervading Viṣṇu and manifests all that was unmanifest.

340. ओं विलासिन्यै नमः

Om vilāsinyai namaḥ

Salutations to Her who is the playful (Lalitā) — Her play being the creation, sustentation and dissolution of the universe.

341. ओं क्षेत्रस्वरूपायै नमः

Om kṣetra-svarūpāyai namaḥ

Salutations to Her who is the body of all beings.

342. ओं क्षेत्रेश्यै नमः

Om kṣetr'eśyai namaḥ

Salutations to Her who is also the ruler of all bodies.

343. ओं क्षेत्र-क्षेत्रज्ञ-पालिन्यै नमः

Om kṣetra-kṣetrajña-pālinyai namaḥ

Salutations to Her who protects both the soul and the body.

344. ओं क्षयवृद्धि-विनिर्मुक्तायै नमः

Om kṣaya-vṛddhi-vinirmuktayai namaḥ

Salutations to Her who is without growth and without decay.

345. ओं क्षेत्रपाल-समर्चितायै नमः

Om kṣetra-pāla-samarcitāyai namaḥ

Salutations to Her who is worshipped by the Kṣetrapāla the keeper of the body (the Jīva).

346. ओं विजयायै नमः

Om vijayāyai namaḥ

Salutations to Her who is the victorious.

347. ओं विमलायै नमः

Om vimalāyai namaḥ

Salutations to Her who is Vimalā or the Pure.

348. ओं वन्द्यायै नमः

Om vandyāyai namaḥ

Salutations to Her who is the adorable.

349. ओं वन्दारु-जन-वत्सलायै नमः

Om vandāru-jana-vatsalāyai namaḥ

Salutations to Her who loves devotees like a mother.

350. ओं वाग्वादिन्यै नमः

Om vāg-vādinyai namaḥ

Salutations to Her who is vāg-vādinī or the power that prompts holy men to speak words of wisdom.

351. ओं वामकेश्यै नमः

Om vāma-keśyai namaḥ

Salutations to Her who is Vāmakeśī or one with lovely locks of hair.

352. ओं वह्निमण्डल-वासिन्यै नमः

Om vahni-maṇḍala-vāsinyai namaḥ

Salutations to Her who lives in a circle of fire.

353. ओं भक्तिमत्-कल्पलतिकायै नमः

Om bhaktimat-kalpa-latikāyai namaḥ

Salutations to Her who is verily a Kalpa Taru, the wish-yielding tree of Heaven that grants all the prayers of devotees.

354. ओं पशुपाश-विमोचिन्यै नमः

Om paśu-pāśa-vimocinyai namaḥ

Salutations to Her who releases the ignorant from their bond of ignorance.

355. ओं संहृताशेष-पाषण्डायै नमः

Om samhṛtāśeṣa-pāṣaṇḍāyai namaḥ

Salutations to Her the destroyer of heretics -those who are averse to spiritual values.

356. ओं सदाचार-प्रवर्तिकायै नमः

Om sadācāra-pravartikāyai namaḥ

Salutations to Her who inspires men to right conduct.

357. ओं तापत्रयाग्नि - संतप्त - समाह्लादन - चन्द्रिकायै मनः

Om tāpa - tray'āgni - santapta
sam'āhlādana - candrikāyai namaḥ

Salutations to Her who is like moonlight that gives joy to those who are burnt by the triple fires of misery—those generated by physical, mental and supernatural causes.

358. ओं तरुण्यै नमः

Om taruṇyai namaḥ

Salutations to Her who is ever young.

359. ओं तापसाराध्यायै नमः

Om tāpas'ārādhyāyai namaḥ

Salutations to Her who is adored by ascetics.

360. ओं तनुमध्यायै नमः

Om tanu - madhyāyai namaḥ

Salutations to Her who is Tanu - madhyā the Deity who is slender in the waist.

361. ओं तमोपहायै नमः

Om tam'opahāyai namaḥ

Salutations to Her who is the dispeller of ignorance in aspirants.

362. ओं चित्यै नमः

Om cityai namaḥ

Salutations to Her who is Citi, the independent power that sustains everything.

363. ओं तत्पद - लक्ष्यार्थायै नमः

Om tat - pada - lakṣ'yārthāyai namaḥ

Salutations to Her who is denoted by the word Tat (That).

364. ओं चिदेकरस - रूपिण्यै नमः

Om cid - eka - rasa - rūpiṇyai namaḥ

Salutations to Her who is of the nature of Pure Consciousness.

365. ओं स्वात्मानन्द - लवीभूत - ब्रह्माद्यानन्द - सन्तत्यै: नम:

*Om sv'ātm'ānandalavī - bhūta-
brah'mādyānanda - santatyai namaḥ*

Salutations to Her a fraction of whose bliss forms the bliss manifest in Brahmā and others.

366. ओं परायै नम:

Om parāyai namaḥ

Salutations to Her who is the Parā or the Transcendent Word (above the other lower stages of speech known as Paśyantī, Madhyamā and Vaikharī).

367. ओं प्रत्यक् - चितीरूपायै नम:

Om pratyak - citī - rūpāyai namaḥ

Salutations to Her who is in the form of consciousness turned inward (when the Reality is unmanifest in dissolution).

368. ओं पश्यन्त्यै नम:

Om paśyantyai namaḥ

Salutations to Her who is Paśyantī, or speech in the inaudible stage.

369. ओं परदेवतायै नमः

Om para - devatāyai namaḥ

Salutations to Her who is Paradevatā the object of supreme devotion.

370. ओं मध्यमायै नमः

Om madhyamāyai namaḥ

Salutations to Her who is Madhyamā, or speech in the middle stage of its external expressions.

371. ओं वैखरी - रूपायै नमः

Om vaikharī - rūpāyai namaḥ

Salutations to Her who is Vaikharī the uttered audible speech.

372. ओं भक्त - मानस - हंसिकायै नमः

Om bhakta - mānasa - hamsikāyai namaḥ

Salutations to Her who is the swan sporting in the Mānasā lake of Her devotees' minds.

373. ओं कामेश्वर - प्राणनाड्यै नमः

Om kāmeśvara - prāṇa - nāḍyai namaḥ

Salutations to Her who is the very life of Her Consort Kāmeśvara.

374. ओं कृतज्ञायै नमः

Om kṛtajñāyai namaḥ

Salutations to Her who knows all that men do.

375. ओं कामपूजितायै नमः

Om kāma - pūjitāyai namaḥ

Salutations to Her who is adored by Manmatha the god of love (or who dwells in the Mulādhāra Cakra).

376. ओं शृंगार - रस - संपूर्णायै नमः

Om śṛṅgāra - rasa - sampūrṇāyai namaḥ

Salutations to Her who is the essence of Love (or who lives where love in fullness is found).

377. ओं जयायै नमः

Om jayāyai namaḥ

Salutations to Her who is designated as the victorious one.

378. ओं जालंधर - स्थितायै नमः

Om jālandhara - sthitāyai namaḥ

Salutations to Her who is Viṣṇumukhī at the holy shrine of Jālandhara (or who dwells in Viśuddhi Cakra).

379. ओं ओड्याण - पीठ - निलयायै नमः

Om oḍyāṇa - pīṭha - nilayāyai namaḥ

Salutations to Her who is present at holy seat or Oḍyāṇa (or who dwells in the Ājñā Cakra).

380. ओं बिन्दु - मण्डलवासिन्यै नमः

Om bindu - maṇḍala - vāsinyai namaḥ

Salutations to Her who dwells in the Brahmarandhra of the individual.

381. ओं रहोयाग - क्रमाराध्यायै नमः

Om raho - yāga - kram'ārādhyāyai namaḥ

Salutations to Her who is to be worshipped by secret rites.

382. ओं रहस्तर्पण - तर्पितायै नमः

Om rahas - tarpaṇa - tarpitāyai namaḥ

Salutations to Her who is gratified by secret libations.

383. ओं सद्यःप्रसादिन्यै नमः

Om sadyaḥ - prasādinyai namaḥ

Salutations to Her who bestows Her grace immediately on being so worshipped.

384. ओं विश्वसाक्षिण्यै नमः

Om viśva - sākṣiṇyai namaḥ

Salutations to Her who is the witness of everything.

385. ओं साक्षिवर्जितायै नमः

Om sākṣi - varjitāyai namaḥ

Salutations to Her who has Herself no witness.

386. ओं षडंगदेवता - युक्तायै नमः

Om ṣaḍaṅga - devatā - yuktāyai namaḥ

Salutations to Her who is accompanied by the deities of the six Aṅgas (parts—heart, head, hair, eyes, armour and weapons).

387. ओं षाड्गुण्य - परिपूरितायै नमः

Om ṣāḍguṇya - pari - pūritāyai namaḥ

Salutations to Her who is endowed with the six good qualities in perfection.

388. ओं नित्य - क्लिन्नायै नमः

Om nitya - klinnāyai namaḥ

Salutations to Her who is ever compassionate.

389. ओं निरुपमायै नमः

Om nirupamāyai namaḥ

Salutations to Her who is peerless.

390. ओं निर्वाण - सुख - दायिन्यै नमः

Om nirvāṇa - sukha - dāyinyai namaḥ

Salutations to Her who confers the bliss of Nirvāṇa.

391. ओं नित्याषोडशिका - रूपायै नमः

Om nityā - ṣoḍaśikā - rūpāyai namaḥ

Salutations to Her who is in the form of the sixteen Nityas (Tripurasundarī with Her companions).

392. ओं श्रीकण्ठार्ध - शरीरिण्यै नमः

Om śrīkaṇṭhārdha - śarīriṇyai namaḥ

Salutations to Her who has a body constituting the half of Śiva.

393. ओं प्रभावत्यै नमः

Om prabhāvatyai namaḥ

Salutations to Her who is endowed with the power of effulgence (Prabhāvatī).

394. ओं प्रभारूपायै नमः

Om prabhā - rūpāyai namaḥ

Salutations to Her who is the Effulgence of Power itself.

395. ओं प्रसिद्धायै नमः

Om prasiddhāyai namaḥ

Salutations to Her who is the celebrated.

396. ओं परमेश्वर्यै नमः

Om parameśvaryai namaḥ

Salutations to Her who is the Sovereign Supreme.

397. ओं मूलप्रकृत्यै नमः

Om mūla - prakṛtyai namaḥ

Salutations to Her who is the first cause.

398. ओं अव्यक्तायै नमः

Om avyaktāyai namaḥ

Salutations to Her who is the unmanifest state of the universe.

399. ओं व्यक्ताव्यक्त - स्वरूपिण्यै नमः

Om vyakt'āvyakta - svarūpiṇyai namaḥ

Salutations to Her who is the manifest and the unmanifest states.

400. ओं व्यापिन्यै नमः

Om vyāpinyai namaḥ

Salutations to Her who is all - pervading.

401. ओं विविधाकारायै नमः

Om vividh'ākārāyai namaḥ

Salutations to Her who has many forms.

402. ओं विद्याविद्या - स्वरूपिण्यै नमः

Om vidy'āvidyā - svarūpiṇyai namaḥ

Salutations to Her who is both Knowledge and Ignorance.

403. ओं महाकामेश - नयन - कुमुदाह्लाद - कौमुद्यै नमः

*Om mahā - kāmeśa - nayana-
kumud'āhlāda - kaumudyai namaḥ*

Salutations to Her who gladdens the eyes of Her Lord Kameśvara as the moon gladdens the water - lilies.

404. ओं भक्त-हार्द-तमो-भेद-भानुमद्भानु-सन्तत्यै नमः

*Om bhakta-hārda - tamo - bheda-
bhānumad - bhānu - santatyai namaḥ*

Salutations to Her who dispels the darkness of ignorance in the minds of devotees as the sun's rays dispel the darkness of the world.

405. ओं शिवदूत्यै नमः

Om śiva - dūtyai namaḥ

Salutations to Her for whom Śiva became the herald.

406. ओं शिवाराध्यायै नमः

Om śiv'ārādhyāyai namaḥ

Salutations to Her who is worshipped by Śiva.

407. ओं शिवमूर्त्यै नमः

Om śiva-mūrtyai namaḥ

Salutations to Her whose form is Śiva.

408. ओं शिवंकर्यै नमः

Om śivaṅkaryai namaḥ

Salutations to Her who dispenses happiness.

409. ओं शिवप्रियायै नमः

Om śiva - priyāyai namaḥ

Salutations to Her who is the beloved of Śiva.

410. ओं शिवपरायै नमः

Om śiva - parāyai namaḥ

Salutations to Her who is solely devoted to Śiva.

411. ओं शिष्टेष्टायै नमः

Om śiṣṭ'eṣṭāyai namaḥ

Salutations to Her who is dear to the righteous.

412. ओं शिष्टपूजितायै नमः

Om śiṣṭa - pūjitāyai namaḥ

Salutations to Her who is adored by the righteous.

413. ओं अप्रमेयायै नमः

Om aprameyāyai namaḥ

Salutations to Her who is the Infinite that is immeasurable.

414. ओं स्वप्रकाशायै नमः

Om svaprakāśāyai namaḥ

Salutations to Her who is self - illumined.

415. ओं मनो - वाचामगोचरायै नमः

Om mano - vācām - agocarāyai namaḥ

Salutations to Her who is beyond the range of mind and speech.

416. ओं चिच्छक्त्यै नमः

Om cicchaktyai namaḥ

Salutations to Her who is the Power of Consciousness.

417. ओं चेतना - रूपायै नमः

Om cetanā - rūpāyai namaḥ

Salutations to Her who is pure consciousness itself.

418. ओं जडशक्त्यै नमः

Om jaḍa - śaktyai namaḥ

Salutations to Her who is manifesting as the mechanical forces.

419. ओं जडात्मिकायै नमः

Om jaḍ'ātmikāyai namaḥ

Salutations to Her who is the innermost essence of all mechanical forces.

420. ओं गायत्र्यै नमः

Om gāyatryai namaḥ

Salutations to Her who is the Gāyatrī Mantra.

421. ओं व्याहृत्यै नमः

Om vyāhṛtyai namaḥ

Salutations to Her who is the seven Vyahṛitis (invocations) of Gāyatrī Mantra.

422. ओं संध्यायै नमः

Om sandhyāyai namaḥ

Salutations to Her who is the Deity for whose adoration the Sandhyā (twilight worship) is done.

423. ओं द्विजवृन्द-निषेवितायै नमः

Om dvija-vrnda-niṣevitāyai namaḥ

Salutations to Her who is adored by holymen at the Sandhyā worship.

424. ओं तत्त्वासनायै नमः

Om tattv'āsanāyai namaḥ

Salutations to Her whose seat is constituted of the Cosmic Elements (the thirty six Tattvas).

425. ओं तस्मै नमः

Om tasmai namaḥ

Salutations to Her who is denoted by the mystic syllable Tat (That).

426. ओं तुभ्यं नमः

Om tubhyam namaḥ

Salutations to Her who is addressed as Tvam (Thou) in prayers and hymns.

427. ओं अय्यै नमः

Om ayyai namaḥ

Salutations to Her who is referred to as Ayi (dear one).

428. ओं पंचकोशान्तर-स्थितायै नमः

Om pañca-kośāntara-sthitāyai namaḥ

Salutations to Her who is the Jīva within the five Kośas (psychological sheaths of the Jīva's personality).

429. ओं निःसीम-महिम्ने नमः

Om niḥsīma-mahimne namaḥ

Salutations to Her whose glory is boundless.

430. ओं नित्य-यौवनायै नमः

Om nitya-yauvanāyai namaḥ

Salutations to Her who is ever youthful.

431. ओं मदशालिन्यै नमः

Om mada-śālinyai namaḥ

Salutations to Her who is ever inebriated with Bliss.

432. ओं मदघूर्णित-रक्ताक्ष्यै नमः

Om mada-ghūrṇita-rakt'ākṣyai namaḥ

Salutations to Her whose red-tinged eyes are turned inward owing to the exuberance of bliss.

433. ओं मदपाटल-गण्डभुवे नमः

Om mada-pāṭala-gaṇḍa-bhuve namaḥ

Salutations to Her whose cheeks are rosy with rapture.

434. ओं चन्दन-द्रव-दिग्धाङ्ग्यै नमः

Om candana-drava-digdhāṅgyai namaḥ

Salutations to Her whose person is fragrant with the scent of sandal paste.

435. ओं चांपेय-कुसुम-प्रियायै नमः

Om cāmpeya-kusuma-priyāyai namaḥ

Salutations to Her who is fond of the fragrant Cāmpa flower.

436. ओं कुशलायै नमः

Om kuśalāyai namaḥ

Salutations to Her who is skilful.

437. ओं कोमलाकारायै नमः

Om komal'ākārāyai namaḥ

Salutations to Her whose form is graceful.

438. ओं कुरुकुल्लायै नमः

Om kurukullāyai namaḥ

Salutations to Her who is the Deity Kurukulla.

439. ओं कुलेश्वर्यै नमः

Om kul'eśvaryai namaḥ

Salutations to Her who is the ruler of the Kula (Suṣumnā).

440. ओं कुलकुण्डालयायै नमः

Om kula-kuṇḍ'ālayāyai namaḥ

Salutations to Her who is the Deity in the Kulakuṇḍa (the Mūlādhāra).

441. ओं कौल्मार्ग - तत्पर - सेवितायै नमः

Om kaula - mārga - tatpara - sevitāyai namaḥ

Salutations to Her who is worshipped by those who are devoted to the Kaula tradition.

442. ओं कुमार - गणनाथांबायै नमः

Om kumāra - gaṇanāth'āmbāyai namaḥ

Salutations to Her who is the Mother of Kumāra and Gaṇanātha.

443. ओं तुष्ट्यै नमः

Om tuṣṭyai namaḥ

Salutations to Her who is contentment, (Tuṣṭi) and is also worshipped as the deity Tuṣṭi.

444. ओं पुष्ट्यै नमः

Om puṣṭyai namaḥ

Salutations to Her who is fulness (Puṣṭi) and is also the deity Puṣṭi.

445. ओं मत्यै नमः

Om matyai namaḥ

Salutations to Her who is wisdom (mati) and is also worshipped as the deity Mati.

446. ओं धृत्यै नमः

Om dhṛtyai namaḥ

Salutations to Her who is fortitude (Dhṛti) and is also worshipped as the deity Dhṛti.

447. ओं शान्त्यै नमः

Om śāntyai namaḥ

Salutations to Her who is serenity.

448. ओं स्वस्तिमत्यै नमः

Om svasti matyai namaḥ

Salutations to Her who is benediction.

449. ओं कान्त्यै नमः

Om kāntyai namaḥ

Salutations to Her who is luminosity.

450. ओं नन्दिन्यै नमः

Om nandinyai namaḥ

Salutations to Her who bestows delight.

451. ओं विघ्ननाशिन्यै नमः

Om vighna - nāśinyai namaḥ

Salutations to Her who puts an end to all obstacles.

452. ओं तेजोवत्यै नमः

Om tejovatyai namaḥ

Salutations to Her who is effulgent.

453. ओं त्रिनयनायै नमः

Om tri - nayanāyai namaḥ

Salutations to Her who is endowed with three eyes.

454. ओं लोलाक्षी - कामरूपिण्यैनमः

Om lolākṣī - kāma - rūpiṇyai namaḥ

Salutations to Her who is love in women.

455. ओं मालिन्यै नमः

Om mālinyai namaḥ

Salutations to Her who wears a garland representing the fifty one syllables of the Mātṛkā.

456. ओं हंसिन्यै नमः

Om hamsinyai namaḥ

Salutations to Her who is the Hamsa - mantra (*So'ham Hamsaḥ* reverberating with every breath).

457. ओं मात्रे नमः

Om mātre - namaḥ

Salutations to Her who is the creatrix.

458. ओं मलयाचल - वासिन्यै नमः

Om malay'ācala - vāsinyai namaḥ

Salutations to Her who dwells on the Malaya mountain.

459. ओं सुमुख्यै नमः

Om sumukhyai namaḥ

Salutations to Her who has a lovely face.

460. ओं नलिन्यै नमः

Om nalinyai namaḥ

Salutations to Her who is called Nalinī, because her eyes, limbs etc. have the loveliness of Nalinī or lotus.

461. ओं सुभ्रुवे नमः

Om subhruve namaḥ

Salutations to Her who has attractive eyebrows.

462. ओं शोभनायै नमः

Om śobhanāyai namaḥ

Salutations to Her who is all radiance with beauty.

463. ओं सुरनायिकायै नमः

Om sura - nāyikāyai namaḥ

Salutations to Her who is the leader of the gods.

464. ओं कालकण्ठ्यै नमः

Om kāla - kaṇṭhyai namaḥ

Salutations to Her who is the consort of Kāla - Kaṇṭha (Śiva).

465. ओं कान्तिमत्यै नमः

Om kānti - matyai namaḥ

Salutations to Her who is resplendent.

466. ओं क्षोभिण्यै नमः

Om kṣobhiṇyai namaḥ

Salutations to Her who generates the creative upheaval that causes the evolution of Prakṛti at the beginning of a cycle and fructifies the Karma efficiencies of Jīvas.

467. ओं सूक्ष्मरूपिण्यै नमः

Om sūkṣma - rūpiṇyai namaḥ

Salutations to Her whose form is subtle.

468. ओं वज्रेश्वर्यै नमः

Om vajr'eśvaryai namaḥ

Salutations to Her who is Vajr'eśvarī, the Deity of a holy place known by that name.

469. ओं वामदेव्यै नमः

Om vāma - devyai namaḥ

Salutations to Her who is the consort of Vāmadeva (Śiva).

470. ओं वयोवस्था - विवर्जितायै नमः

Om vayo'vasthā - vivarjitāyai namaḥ

Salutations to Her who is devoid of old age and all other changes.

471. ओं सिद्धेश्वर्यै नमः

Om siddh'eśvaryai namaḥ

Salutations to Her who is the supreme goddess of Siddhas or spiritual adepts.

472. ओं सिद्धविद्यायै नमः

Om siddha - vidyāyai namaḥ

Salutations to Her whose Mantra (Śrīvidyā) is always fruitful.

473. ओं सिद्धमात्रे नमः

Om siddha - mātre namaḥ

Salutations to Her who is the Mother ever ready to help aspirants.

474. ओं यशस्विन्यै नमः

Om yaśasvinyai namaḥ

Salutations to Her who is most renowned.

475. ओं विशुद्धिचक्र - निलयायै नमः

Om viśuddhi - cakra - nilayāyai namaḥ

Salutations to Her who resides in the Viśuddhi Cakra.

476. ओं आरक्तवर्णायै नमः

Om ārakta - varṇāyai namaḥ

Salutations to Her who is of a rosy complexion like the Pāṭali flower.

477. ओं त्रिलोचनायै नमः

Om tri - locanāyai namaḥ

Salutations to Her who has three eyes.

478. ओं खट्वांगादि - प्रहरणायै नमः

Om khaṭvāṅgādi - praharaṇāyai namaḥ

Salutations to Her who is armed with a club and other weapons.

479. ओं वदनैक - समन्वितायै नमः

Om vadan'aika - samanvitāyai namaḥ

Salutations to Her who is with a single face.

480. ओं पायसान्नप्रियायै नमः

Om pāyas'ānna-priyāyai namaḥ

Salutations to Her who likes offerings of Pāyasa (milk pudding).

481. ओं त्वक्स्थायै नमः

Om tvaksthāyai namaḥ

Salutations to Her who presides over the skin that gives the sensation of touch.

482. ओं पशुलोक - भयंकर्यै नमः

Om paśu - loka - bhayankaryai namaḥ

Salutations to Her who is frightful to the ignorant (Paśu).

483. ओं अमृतादि - महाशक्ति - संवृतायै नमः

Om amṛt'ādi - mahā - śakti - samvṛtāyai namaḥ

Salutations to Her who is surrounded by sixteen Śaktis beginning with Amṛta.

484. ओं डाकिनीश्वर्यै नमः

Om dākin'īśvaryai namaḥ

Salutations to Her who is the Divine Ruler Dākinī (described by the nine names from 475 to 483).

485. ओं अनाहताब्ज - निलयायै नमः

Om anāhat'ābja - nilayāyai namaḥ

Salutations to Her who is in the form of the Yoginī called Rākiṇī abiding in the Anāhata Cakra.

486. ओं श्यामाभायै नमः

Om śyām'ābhāyai namaḥ

Salutations to Her who is of shining dark complexion.

487. ओं वदनद्वयायै नमः

Om vadana - dvayāyai namaḥ

Salutations to Her who as Rākiṇī has two faces

488. ओं दंष्ट्रोज्ज्वलायै नमः

Om damṣṭr'ojjvalāyai namaḥ

Salutations to Her who has shining fangs.

489. ओं अक्षमालादि - धरायै नमः

Om akṣa - māl'ādi - dharāyai namaḥ

Salutations to Her who wears a rosary etc.

490. ओं रुधिर - संस्थितायै नमः

Om rudhira - samsthitāyai namaḥ

Salutations to Her who presides over blood in living beings.

491. ओं कालरात्र्यादि - शक्त्यौघ - वृतायै नमः

Om kāla - rātryādi - śakty'augh'āvṛtāyai namaḥ

Salutations to Her who is attended by Kālarātrī and eleven other Śaktis.

492. ओं स्निग्धौदन - प्रियायै नमः

Om snigdh'audana - priyāyai namaḥ

Salutations to Her who loves offerings of rice mixed with ghee.

493. ओं महावीरेन्द्र - वरदायै नमः

Om mahā - vīrendra - varadāyai namaḥ

Salutations to Her who grants boons to great heroes.

494. ओं राकिण्यंबा - स्वरूपिण्यै नमः

Om rākiṇy'ambā - svarūpiṇyai namaḥ

Salutations to Her who is the Mother as Rākiṇī (described in the nine names from 485 to 493).

495. ओं मणिपूराब्ज - निलयायै नमः

Om maṇipūr'ābja - nilayāyai namaḥ

Salutations to Her who resides in the Maṇipūra centre and is known as Lākinī.

496. ओं वदनत्रय - संयुतायै नमः

Om vadana - traya - samyutāyai namaḥ

Salutations to Her who has three faces.

497. ओं वज्रादिकायुधोपेतायै नमः

Oṃ vajr'ādikāyudhopetāyai namaḥ

Salutations to Her who has the thunderbolt and other weapons.

498. ओं डामर्यादिभि - रावृतायै नमः

Om ḍāmary'ādibhir āvṛtāyai namaḥ

Salutations to Her who is surrounded by ten Śaktis beginning with Ḍāmarī.

499. ओं रक्तवर्णायै नमः

Om rakta - varṇāyai namaḥ

Salutations to Her who has a ruddy hue.

500. ओं मांसनिष्ठायै नमः

Om māmsa - niṣṭhāyai namaḥ

Salutations to Her who presides over flesh in living creatures.

501. ओं गुडान्न - प्रीत - मानसायै नमः

Om guḍ'ānna - prīta - mānasāyai namaḥ

Salutations to Her who has a liking for rice cooked with jaggery.

502. ओं समस्तभक्त - सुखदायै नमः

Om samasta - bhakta - sukhadāyai namaḥ

Salutations to Her who bestows happiness on all devotees.

503. ओं लाकिन्यंबा - स्वरूपिण्यै नमः

Om lākiny'ambā - svarūpiṇyai namaḥ

Salutations to Her who is the Mother with the form of Lākinī (described in the nine preceding names from 494 to 502).

504. ओं स्वाधिष्ठानांबुजगतायै नमः

Om svādhiṣṭhān'āmbuja - gatāyai namaḥ

Salutations to Her who abides in the Svādhiṣṭhana Cakra under the name of Kākinī.

505. ओं चतुर्वक्त्र - मनोहरायै नमः

Om catur - vaktra - manoharāyai namaḥ

Salutations to Her who is fascinating with Her four faces.

506. ओं शूलाद्यायुध - संपन्नायै नमः

Om śūlādy'āyudha - sampannāyai namaḥ

Salutations to Her who is armed with a trident and other weapons in Her four hands.

507. ओं पीतवर्णायै नमः

Om pīta - varṇāyai namaḥ

Salutations to Her who is yellow in hue (i.e.golden in colour).

508. ओं अतिगर्वितायै नमः

Om ati - garvitāyai namaḥ

Salutations to Her who is very dignified.

509. ओं मेदो - निष्ठायै नमः

Om medo - niṣṭhāyai namaḥ

Salutations to Her who presides over fatty substances in living beings.

510. ओं मधुप्रीतायै नमः

Om madhu - prītāyai namaḥ

Salutations to Her who loves to have offerings of honey.

511. ओं बन्धिन्यादि - समन्वितायै नमः

Om bandhiny'ādi - samanvitāyai namaḥ

Salutations to Her who is surrounded by Bandhinī and other five Śaktis.

512. ओं दध्यन्नासक्त - हृदयायै नमः

Om dadhy'annāsakta - hṛdayāyai namaḥ

Salutations to Her who loves to have offerings of curd.

513. ओं काकिनी - रूप - धारिण्यै नमः

Om kākinī - rūpa - dhāriṇyai namaḥ

Salutations to the Mother who appears in the form of Kākinī (described in the nine names from 504 to 512).

514. ओं मूलाधारांबुजारूढायै नमः

Om mūlādhār'āmbuj'ārūḍhāyai namaḥ

Salutations to Her who assumes Her place in the Mūlādhāra Cakra, described as a lotus of four petals.

515. ओं पञ्चवक्त्रायै नमः

Om pañca - vaktrāyai namaḥ

Salutations to Her who exhibits five faces.

516. ओं अस्थिसंस्थितायै नमः

Om asthi samsthitāyai namaḥ

Salutations to Her who presides over bones in living creatures.

517. ओं अङ्कुशादि - प्रहरणायै नमः

Om aṅkuś'ādi - praharaṇāyai namaḥ

Salutations to Her who is armed with a goad and other weapons.

518. ओं वरदादि - निषेवितायै नमः

Om varad'ādi - niṣevitāyai namaḥ

Salutations to Her who is attended on by Varadā and three other Śaktis.

519. ओं मुद्गौदनासक्त - चित्तायै नमः

Om mudg'audan'āsakta - cittāyai namaḥ

Salutations to Her who loves offerings of boiled pulse and rice.

520. ओं साकिन्यंबा - स्वरूपिण्यै नमः

Om sākiny'ambā - svarūpiṇyai namaḥ

Salutations to the Mother who appears in the form of Sākinī (described in the six names from 514 to 519).

521. ओं आज्ञा - चक्राब्ज - निलयायै नमः

Om ājñā - cakr'ābja - nilayāyai namaḥ

Salutations to the Mother who resides in the ājñā Cakra (which is described as a lotus with two petals).

522. ओं शुक्लवर्णायै नमः

Om śukla - varṇāyai namaḥ

Salutations to Her who is white in complexion.

523. ओं षडाननायै नमः

Om ṣaḍ - ānanāyai namaḥ

Salutations to Her who has six faces.

524. ओं मज्जा - संस्थायै नमः

Om majjā - samsthāyai namaḥ

Salutations to Her who presides over marrow of living beings.

525. ओं हंसवती - मुख्य - शक्ति - समन्वितायै नमः

Om hamsa - vatī - mukhya - śakti-samanvitāyai namaḥ

Salutations to Her who is attended on by Hamsavatī and other Śaktis.

526. ओं हरिद्रान्नैक - रसिकायै नमः

Om haridr'ānn'aika - rasikāyai namaḥ

Salutations to Her who loves offerings of saffron - flavoured rice.

527. ओं हाकिनी - रूप - धारिण्यै नमः

Om hākinī - rūpa - dhāriṇyai namaḥ

Salutations to the Mother who assumes the form of Hākinī (described in the six names from 521 to 526).

528. ओं सहस्रदल - पद्मस्थायै नमः

Om sahasra - dala - padmasthāyai namaḥ

Salutations to Her who dwells in the Sahasrāra which is described as a thousand petalled lotus.

529. ओं सर्व - वर्णोप - शोभितायै नमः

Om sarva - varṇ'opaśobhitāyai namaḥ

Salutations to Her who shines with all colours.

530. ओं सर्वायुध - धरायै नमः

Om sarv'āyudha - dharāyai namaḥ

Salutations to Her who is armed with all weapons.

531. ओं शुक्ल - संस्थितायै नमः

Om śukla - samsthitāyai namaḥ

Salutations to Her who presides over the vital fluid in all creatures.

532. ओं सर्वतोमुख्यै नमः

Om sarvato'mukhyai namaḥ

Salutations to Her who has faces all round and see in all directions.

533. ओं सर्वौदन - प्रीतचित्तायै नमः

Om sarv'audana - prīta - cittāyai namaḥ

Salutations to Her who loves to have offerings of all kinds of food.

534. ओं याकिन्यंबा - स्वरूपिण्यै नमः

Om yākiny'ambā - svarūpiṇyai namaḥ

Salutations to the Mother who appears in the form of Yākinī (described in the six names from 528 to 533).

535. ओं स्वाहायै नमः

Om svāhāyai namaḥ

Salutations to Her who is the deity of Svāhā, the sacred exclamation with which oblations are made in sacrificial fire for gods.

536. ओं स्वधायै नमः

Om svadhāyai namaḥ

Salutations to the Deity Svadhā, the sacred exclamation uttered while making oblations to the Pitṛs (manes).

537. ओं अमत्यै नमः

Om amatyai namaḥ

Salutations to Her who is Amati (Buddhi or knowledge).

538. ओं मेधायै नमः

Om medhāyai namaḥ

Salutations to Her who has become intelligence.

539. ओं श्रुत्यै नमः

Om śrutyai namaḥ

Salutations to Her who is the śruti or the Veda.

540. ओं स्मृत्यै नमः

Om smṛtyai namaḥ

Salutations to Her who has become memory.

541. ओं अनुत्तमायै नमः

Om anuttamāyai namaḥ

Salutations to Her who has none superior.

542. ओं पुण्यकीर्त्यै नमः

Om puṇya - kīrtyai namaḥ

Salutations to Her who is famed for holiness.

543. ओं पुण्यलभ्यायै नमः

Om puṇya - labhyāyai namaḥ

Salutations to Her who can be attained only through holiness.

544. ओं पुण्यश्रवण - कीर्तनायै नमः

Om puṇya - śravaṇa - kīrtanāyai namaḥ

Salutations to Her to hear of whom and to praise whom make for holiness.

545. ओं पुलोमजार्चितायै नमः

Om pulomaj'ārcitāyai namaḥ

Salutations to Her who is adored by Pulomajā, the consort of Indra.

546. ओं बन्धमोचन्यै नमः

Om bandha - mocanyai namaḥ

Salutations to Her who liberates the Jīva from the bondage of Samsāra.

547. ओं बर्बरालकायै नमः

Om barbar'ālakāyai namaḥ

Salutations to Her who is wavy - haired.

548. ओं विमर्शरूपिण्यै नमः

Om vimarśa - rūpiṇyai namaḥ

Salutations to Her who is of the nature of Vimarśa , the mirror of objectivity which makes Śiva self - aware as Prakāśa (the pure Luminosity), the subject.

549. ओं विद्यायै नमः

Om vidyāyai namaḥ

Salutations to Her who is Vidyā, the knowledge that gives spiritual enlightenment.

550. ओं वियदादि - जगत्प्रसुवे नमः

Om viyad'ādi - jagat - prasuve namaḥ

Salutations to Her who is the origin of the whole cosmos beginning with the element of Ākāśa (space).

551. ओं सर्वव्याधि - प्रशमन्यै नमः

Om sarva - vyādhi - praśamanyai namaḥ

Salutations to Her who cures all ills.

552. ओं सर्वमृत्यु - निवारिण्यै नमः

Om sarva - mṛtyu - nivāriṇyai namaḥ

Salutations to Her who wards off all forms of death.

553. ओं अग्रगण्यायै नमः

Om agra - gaṇyāyai namaḥ

Salutations to Her who is to be reckoned as the First in everything.

554. ओं अचिन्त्यरूपायै नमः

Om acintya - rūpāyai namaḥ

Salutations to Her who transcends all thought.

555. ओं कलिकल्मष - नाशिन्यै नमः

Om kali - kalmaṣa - nāśinyai namaḥ

Salutations to Her who destroys the sins of the degenerate age of Kali.

556. ओं कात्यायन्यै नमः

Om kātyāyanyai namaḥ

Salutations to Her who is Kātyāyanī, the sumtotal of the effulgence of all the Deities.

557. ओं कालहन्त्र्यै नमः

Om kāla - hantryai namaḥ

Salutations to Her who puts an end to Time, the destroyer of all.

558. ओं कमलाक्ष - निषेवितायै नमः

Om kamalākṣa - niṣevitāyai namaḥ

Salutations to Her who is worshipped even by the lotus - eyed Viṣṇu.

559. ओं तांबूल - पूरित - मुख्यै नमः

Om tāmbūla - pūrita-mukhyai namaḥ

Salutations to Her whose mouth is full of chewing betel.

560. ओं दाडिमी - कुसुम - प्रभायै नमः

Om dāḍimī - kusuma - prabhāyai namaḥ

Salutations to Her who shines like a pomegranate flower.

561. ओं मृगाक्ष्यै नमः

Om mṛgākṣyai namaḥ

Salutations to Her whose eyes are like those of a doe.

562. ओं मोहिन्यै नमः

Om mohinyai namaḥ

Salutations to Her who is of bewitching beauty.

563. ओं मुख्यायै नमः

Om mukhyāyai namaḥ

Salutations to Her who is known as Mukhya - prāṇa, the first - born of creation (known as Hiraṇyagarbha or the four - faced Brahmā).

564. ओं मृडान्यै नमः

Om mṛḍānyai namaḥ

Salutations to Her who is the Consort of Mṛḍa, the Divine dispenser of Happiness (i.e.Śiva in His Sāttvika aspect).

565. ओं मित्ररूपिण्यै नमः

Om mitra - rūpiṇyai namaḥ

Salutations to Her who is effulgent like the sun.

566. ओं नित्य - तृप्तायै नमः

Om nitya - tṛptāyai namaḥ

Salutations to Her who is eternally contented and happy.

567. ओं भक्तनिधये नमः

Om bhakta - nidhaye namaḥ

Salutations to Her who is a treasure to Her devotees.

568. ओं नियन्त्र्यै नमः

Om niyantryai namaḥ

Salutations to Her who is the guide and controller of all.

569. ओं निखिलेश्वर्यै नमः

Om nikhil'eśvaryai namaḥ

Salutations to Her who is Ruler of the worlds.

570. ओं मैत्र्यादि-वासनालभ्यायै नमः

Om maitry'ādi - vāsanā - labhyāyai namaḥ

Salutations to Her who is attained through loving kindness and other such dispositions.

571. ओं महा - प्रलय - साक्षिण्यै नमः

Om mahā - pralaya - sākṣiṇyai namaḥ

Salutations to Her who witnesses the dissolution of the whole cosmos.

572. ओं परस्यै शक्त्यै नमः

Om parasyai śaktyai namaḥ

Salutations to Her who is Parā - śakti, the Supreme Power.

573. ओं परायै निष्ठायै नमः

Om parāyai niṣṭāyai namaḥ

Salutations to Her who is the Supreme End and establishment in Faith.

574. ओं प्रज्ञानघन - रूपिण्यै नमः

Om prajñāna - ghana - rūpiṇyai namaḥ

Salutations to Her who is Pure Consciousness condensed.

575. ओं माध्वीपानालसायै नमः

Om mādhvī - pān'ālasāyai namaḥ

Salutations to Her who is introverted and inactive like one intoxicated with wine.

576. ओं मत्तायै नमः

Om mattāyai namaḥ

Salutations to Her who is the ego - consciousness of Śiva.

577. ओं मातृका - वर्ण - रूपिण्यै नमः

Om mātṛkā - varṇa - rūpiṇyai namaḥ

Salutations to Her to whom all the alphabets are related as Her form.

578. ओं महाकैलास - निलयायै नमः

Om mahā - kailāsa - nilayāyai namaḥ

Salutations to Her whose abode is the Mahā - kailāsa (the Bindu in the Sahasrāra).

579. ओं मृणाल - मृदु - दोर्लतायै नमः

Om mṛṇāla - mṛdu - dor - latāyai namaḥ

Salutations to Her whose arms are smooth and slender like a pair of lotus stalks.

580. ओं महनीयायै नमः

Om mahanīyāyai namaḥ

Salutations to Her who is adorable.

581. ओं दयामूर्त्यै नमः

Om dayā - mūrtyai namaḥ

Salutations to Her who is compassion itself.

582. ओं महासाम्राज्य - शालिन्यै नमः

Om mahā - sāmrājya - śālinyai namaḥ

Salutations to Her to whom belongs the vast empire of the whole universe.

583. ओं आत्मविद्यायै नमः

Om ātma - vidyāyai namaḥ

Salutations to Her who is Ātma - vidyā, the doctrine of the Self.

584. ओं महाविद्यायै नमः

Om mahāvidyāyai namaḥ

Salutations to Her who is Mahā - vidyā, the great doctrine (also a deity).

585. ओं श्रीविद्यायै नमः

Om śrī - vidyāyai namaḥ

Salutations to Her who is Śrī - vidyā (the fifteen lettered Mantra of the Devi).

586. ओं कामसेवितायै नमः

Om kāma - sevitāyai namaḥ

Salutations to Her who is meditated upon by Kāmadeva, the god of love.

587. ओं श्रीषोडशाक्षरीविद्यायै नमः

Om śrī - ṣoḍaśākṣarī - vidyāyai namaḥ

Salutations to Her who is the Ṣoḍaśākṣarī - vidyā, the sixteen lettered Mantra of the Devi.

588. ओं त्रिकूटायै नमः

Om trikūṭāyai namaḥ

Salutations to Her who forms the three Kūṭas or groups of letters of Śrī - vidyā.

589. ओं कामकोटिकायै नमः

Om kāma - koṭikāyai namaḥ

Salutations to Her of whom Kāmeśvara (Parama - Śiva) is a mode.

590. ओं कटाक्ष-किंङ्करी-भूत-कमला-कोटि-सेवितायै नमः

Om kaṭākṣa - kiṅkarī - bhūta - kamalā - koṭi - sevitāyai namaḥ

Salutations to Her who can at a mere glance make crores of Lakṣmis (goddesses of wealth and beauty)wait upon Her.

591. ओं शिरस्थितायै नमः

Om śiraḥ - sthitāyai namaḥ

Salutations to Her who dwells in the Sahasrāra in the head.

592. ओं चन्द्रनिभायै नमः

Om candra - nibhāyai namaḥ

Salutations to Her who shines as the Moon in the pericap of the Sahasrāra lotus.

593. ओं भालस्थायै नमः

Om bhālasthāyai namaḥ

Salutations to Her who dwells as the Bindu in the syllable Hrīm meditated in the forehead.

594. ओं इन्द्र - धनुः - प्रभायै नमः

Om indra - dhanuṣ - prabhāyai namaḥ

Salutations to Her who shines in the colours of the rainbow.

595. ओं हृदयस्थायै नमः

Om hṛdayasthāyai namaḥ

Salutations to Her who abides in the heart of the devotees for meditation.

596. ओं रविप्रख्यायै नमः

Om ravi - prakhyāyai namaḥ

Salutations to Her who blazes in the heart like the sun.

597. ओं त्रिकोणान्तर - दीपिकायै नमः

Om tri - koṇāntara - dīpikāyai namaḥ

Salutations to Her who resides in the centre of the Mūlādhāra known as the Trikoṇa.

598. ओं दाक्षायण्यै नमः

Om dākṣāyaṇyai namaḥ

Salutations to Her who manifested as the daughter of Dakṣa.

599. ओं दैत्यहन्त्र्यै नमः

Om daitya - hantryai namaḥ

Salutations to Her who destroys demons who embody the forces of evil.

600. ओं दक्षयज्ञविनाशिन्यै नमः

Om dakṣa - yajña - vināśinyai namaḥ

Salutations to Her who destroyed the sacrifice of Dakṣa.

601. ओं दरान्दोलित - दीर्घाक्ष्यै नमः

Om dar'āndolita - dīrgh'ākṣyai namaḥ

Salutations to Her who has shapely, wide and elongated eyes tremulous with mercy.

602. ओं दरहासोज्ज्वलन्मुख्यै नमः

Om dara - hās'ojjvalan - mukhyai namaḥ

Salutations to Her whose face is lit with a gentle smile.

603. ओं गुरु-मूर्तये नमः

Om guru - mūrtaye namaḥ

Salutations to Her who assumes the form of the Guru.

604. ओं गुणनिधये नमः

Om guṇa - nidhaye namaḥ

Salutations to Her who is a treasure house of virtues.

605. ओं गोमात्रे नमः

Om go - mātre namaḥ

Salutations to Her who is the source of speech.

606. ओं गुहजन्मभुवे नमः

Om guha - janma - bhuve namaḥ

Salutations to Her who is the mother of Guha(Kārtikeya).

607. ओं देवेश्यै नमः

Om deveśyai namaḥ

Salutations to Her who is the ruler of all divinities.

608. ओं दण्डनीतिस्थायै नमः

Om daṇḍa - nītisthāyai namaḥ

Salutations to Her who sits on the throne of justice.

609. ओं दहराकाश - रूपिण्यै नमः

Om dahar'ākāśa - rūpiṇyai namaḥ

Salutations to Her who is the subtle Self in the heart of man.

610. ओं प्रतिपन्मुख्य-राकान्त-तिथि-मण्डल-पूजितायै नमः

Om pratipan - mukhya - rākānta - tithi -

maṇḍala - pūjitāyai namaḥ

Salutations to Her who is to be worshipped on the full - moon day, which is the last day (Tithi) of the lunar fortnight beginning with Pratipada.

611. ओं कलात्मिकायै नमः

Om kal'ātmikāyai namaḥ

Salutations to Her who is Herself all the phases(kalas)of the moon.

612. ओं कलानाथायै नमः

Om kalā - nāthāyai namaḥ

Salutations to Her who is the mistress of all the kalas.

613. ओं काव्यालाप - विमोदिन्यै नमः

Om kāvy'ālāpa - vimodinyai namaḥ

Salutations to Her who delights in the language of poetry.

614. ओं सचामर - रमा - वाणी - सव्य - दक्षिण - सेवितायै नमः

Om sacāmara - ramā - vāṇī - savya - dakṣiṇa - sevitāyai namaḥ

Salutations to Her who is served by Lakṣmi

and Sarasvati standing on Her left and right sides holding Chowri fans.

615. ओं आदिशक्त्यै नमः

Om ādiśaktyai namaḥ

Salutations to Her who is the Ādiśakti or Primordial Power which creates every thing and pervades every thing.

616. ओं अमेयायै नमः

Om ameyāyai namaḥ

Salutations to Her whose greatness is immeasurable.

617. ओं आत्मने नमः

Om ātmane namaḥ

Salutations to Her who is the Self in all.

618. ओं परमायै नमः

Om paramāyai namaḥ

Salutations to Her who is also the Supreme Self.

619. ओं पावनाकृतये नमः

Om pāvan'ākṛtaye namaḥ

Salutations to Her whose form is holy and sanctifying.

620. ओं अनेक-कोटि-ब्रह्माण्ड-जनन्यै नमः

Om aneka - koṭi - brahmāṇḍa - jananyai namaḥ

Salutations to Her who has given birth to several crores of world systems.

621. ओं दिव्य - विग्रहायै नमः

Om divya - vigrahāyai namaḥ

Salutations to Her who has a Divine form.

622. ओं क्लींकार्यै नमः

Om klīṅkāryai namaḥ

Salutations to Her who is represented by the holy syllable *klīm*, known as the Kāmarāja Bīja.

623. ओं केवलायै नमः

Om kevalāyai namaḥ

Salutations to Her who is the Absolute devoid of all attributes.

624. ओं गुह्यायै नमः

Om guhyāyai namaḥ

Salutations to Her who is worshipped in secrecy by some adepts.

625. ओं कैवल्य - पद - दायिन्यै नमः

Om kaivalya - pada - dāyinyai namaḥ

Salutations to Her who confers Kaivalya, the state of Absolute Bliss.

626. ओं त्रिपुरायै नमः

Om tripurāyai namaḥ

Salutations to Her who is Tripurā or the One with three aspects.

627. ओं त्रिजगद्वन्द्यायै नमः

Om trijagad - vandyāyai namaḥ

Salutations to Her who is adored by all in the three worlds.

628. ओं त्रिमूर्तये नमः

Om tri - mūrtaye namaḥ

Salutations to Her who has the three forms of Brahmā, Viṣṇu and Maheśvara.

629. ओं त्रिदशेश्वर्यै नमः

Om tridaśeśvaryai namaḥ

Salutations to Her who is the Mistress governing the Divinities (Tridaśas).

630. ओं त्र्यक्षर्यै नमः

Om tryakṣaryai namaḥ

Salutations to Her who is the Mantra of three parts (Pañcadaśī Mantra of Śrīvidyā).

631. ओं दिव्य - गन्धाढ्यायै नमः

Om divya - gandh'āḍhyāyai namaḥ

Salutations to Her who is full of divine fragrance.

632. ओं सिन्दूर - तिलकांचितायै नमः

Om sindūra - tilak'āñcitāyai namaḥ

Salutations to Her who is adorned with the vermilion mark on the forehead.

633. ओं उमायै नमः

Om umāyai namaḥ

Salutations to Her who is Umā-- Brahma - vidyā personified.

634. ओं शैलेन्द्रतनयायै नमः

Om śailendra - tanayāyai namaḥ

Salutations to Her who is the daughter of the King of Mountains, the Himalayas.

635. ओं गौर्यै नमः

Om gauryai namaḥ

Salutations to Her who is Gaurī, the fair complexioned one.

636. ओं गन्धर्व - सेवितायै नमः

Om gandharva - sevitāyai namaḥ

Salutations to Her who is attended upon by Gandharvas, the celestial minstrels.

637. ओं विश्वगर्भायै नमः

Om viśva - garbhāyai namaḥ

Salutations to Her who has the universe in her womb.

638. ओं स्वर्णगर्भायै नमः

Om ṣvarṇa - garbhāyai namaḥ

Salutations to Her who has everything wholesome and charming hidden within her.

639. ओं अवरदायै नमः

Om avaradāyai namaḥ

Salutations to Her who defeats the ignoble demons.

640. ओं वागधीश्वर्यै नमः

Om vāg - adhīśvaryai namaḥ

Salutations to Her who presides over speech.

641. ओं ध्यानगम्यायै नमः

Om dhyāna - gamyāyai namaḥ

Salutations to Her who can be approached through meditation.

642. ओं अपरिच्छेद्यायै नमः

Om apari - cchedyāyai namaḥ

Salutations to Her who is the Infinite without any limitation.

643. ओं ज्ञानदायै नमः

Om jñānadāyai namaḥ

Salutations to Her who is the giver of Supreme Knowledge.

644. ओं ज्ञानविग्रहायै नमः

Om jñāna - vigrahāyai namaḥ

Salutations to Her who is Herself the embodiment of Supreme Knowledge.

645. ओं सर्व - वेदान्त - संवेद्यायै नमः

Om sarva - vedānta - samvedyāyai namaḥ

Salutations to Her whom all the Vedāntas (Upaniṣads) declare.

646. ओं सत्यानन्द - स्वरूपिण्यै नमः

Om saty'ānanda - svarūpiṇyai namaḥ

Salutations to Her who is Supreme Knowledge and Supreme Bliss.

647. ओं लोपामुद्रार्चितायै नमः

Om lopāmudr'ārcitāyai namaḥ

Salutations to Her who is worshipped through the Mantra named after Lopāmudrā.

648. ओं लीलाक्लृप्त - ब्रह्माण्ड - मण्डलायै नमः

Om līlā - klpta - brahmāṇḍa - maṇḍalāyai namaḥ

Salutations to Her for whom the creation of many a universe is a mere sport.

649. ओं अदृश्यायै नमः

Om adṛśyāyai namaḥ

Salutations to Her who is not an object of ordinary vision.

650. ओं दृश्यरहितायै नमः

Om dṛśya - rahitāyai namaḥ

Salutations to Her who is beyond objectivity.

651. ओं विज्ञात्र्यै नमः

Om vijñātryai namaḥ

Salutations to Her who is the ultimate subject.

652. ओं वेद्य - वर्जितायै नमः

Om vedya - varjitāyai namaḥ

Salutations to Her who, being omniscient, has nothing more to know.

653. ओं योगिन्यै नमः

Om yoginyai namaḥ

Salutations to Her who is Yoginī.

654. ओं योगदायै नमः

Om yogadāyai namaḥ

Salutations to Her who can bestow Yoga to votaries.

655. ओं योग्यायै नमः

Om yogyāyai namaḥ

Salutations to Her who is the object of Yoga.

656. ओं योगानन्दायै नमः

Om yogānandāyai namaḥ

Salutations to Her who is the bliss realised through Yoga.

657. ओं युगन्धरायै नमः

Om yugandharāyai namaḥ

Salutations to Her who bears the Yoke of

Yoga consisting in regulating the evolution during vast periods of time (Yugas).

658. ओं इच्छाशक्ति-ज्ञानशक्ति-क्रियाशक्ति-स्वरूपिण्यै नमः

Om icchā - śakti - jñāna - śakti - kriyā - śakti - svarūpiṇyai namaḥ

Salutations to Her who is the Power of Will (Icchā - śakti), Power of Knowledge (Jñāna - śakti) and Power of Action (kriyā - śakti).

659. ओं सर्वाधारायै नमः

Om sarv'ādhārāyai namaḥ

Salutations to Her on whom everything rests.

660. ओं सुप्रतिष्ठायै नमः

Om supratiṣṭhāyai namaḥ

Salutations to Her who is the firm foundation of all existence.

661. ओं सदसद्रूप - धारिण्यै नमः

Om sad - asad - rūpa - dhāriṇyai namaḥ

Salutations to Her who takes the forms of both Being and Non - being.

662. ओं अष्टमूर्त्यै नमः

Om aṣṭa - mūrtyai namaḥ

Salutations to Her who has an eightfold form.

663. ओं अजाजेत्र्यै नमः

Om ajā jetryai namaḥ

Salutations to Her who helps to overcome Ajā (Ignorance).

664. ओं लोकयात्रा - विधायिन्यै नमः

Om loka - yātrā - vidhāyinyai namaḥ

Salutations to Her who directs the cosmic process.

665. ओं एकाकिन्यै नमः

Om ekākinyai namaḥ

Salutations to Her who is the Alone.

666. ओं भूमरूपायै नमः

Om bhūma - rūpāyai namaḥ

Salutations to Her who is Infinite by nature.

667. ओं निर्द्वैतायै नमः

Om nirdvaitāyai namaḥ

Salutations to Her who has no opposite.

668. ओं द्वैतवर्जितायै नमः

Om dvaita - varjitāyai namaḥ

Salutations to Her who is without any duality.

669. ओं अन्नदायै नमः

Om annadāyai namaḥ

Salutations to Her who supplies food to all.

670. ओं वसुदायै नमः

Om vasudāyai namaḥ

Salutations to Her who is the generous giver of everything valuable.

671. ओं वृद्धायै नमः

Om vṛddhāyai namaḥ

Salutations to Her who is the Primeval One.

672. ओं ब्रह्मात्मैक्य - स्वरूपिण्यै नमः

Om brahm'ātmaikya - svarūpiṇyai namaḥ

Salutations to Her who is the symbol of the oneness of Brahman and the Ātman.

673. ओं बृहत्यै नमः

Om bṛhatyai namaḥ

Salutations to Her who is the Immense.

674. ओं ब्राह्मण्यै नमः

Om brāhmaṇyai namaḥ

Salutations to Her who is the wisdom of the Eternal.

675. ओं ब्राह्म्यै नमः

Om brāhmyai namaḥ

Salutations to Her who belongs to the Eternal.

676. ओं ब्रह्मानन्दायै नमः

Om brahm'ānandāyai namaḥ

Salutations to Her who is the bliss of Brahman.

677. ओं बलिप्रियायै नमः

Om bali - priyāyai namaḥ

Salutations to Her who loves the offerings of devotees.

678. ओं भाषारूपायै नमः

Om bhāṣā - rūpāyai namaḥ

Salutations to Her who is in the form of language.

679. ओं बृहत्सेनायै नमः

Om bṛhat - senāyai namaḥ

Salutations to Her who leads a mighty army.

680. ओं भावाभाव - विवर्जितायै नमः

Om bhāv'ābhāva - vivarjitāyai namaḥ

Salutations to Her who is beyond being and non - being.

681. ओं सुखाराध्यायै नमः

Om sukh'ārādhyāyai namaḥ

Salutations to Her whose worship is easy to perform.

682. ओं शुभकर्यै नमः

Om śubha - karyai namaḥ

Salutations to Her who is blissful in blessing.

683. ओं शोभनायैसुलभायैगत्यै नमः

Om śobhanāyai sulabhāyai gatyai namaḥ

Salutations to Her whose path is lustrous and easy to traverse.

684. ओं राजराजेश्वर्यै नमः

Om rāja - rāj'eśvaryai namaḥ

Salutations to Her who is Rājarājesvarī (the Ruler of rulers).

685. ओं राज्यदायिन्यै नमः

Om rājya - dāyinyai namaḥ

Salutations to Her who bestows dominion.

686. ओं राज्यवल्लभायै नमः

Om rājya - vallabhāyai namaḥ

Salutations to Her who loves dominion.

687. ओं राजत्कृपायै नमः

Om rājat - kṛpāyai namaḥ

Salutations to Her who is gloriously compassionate.

688. ओं राजपीठ - निवेशित - निजाश्रितायै नमः

Om rāja - pīṭha - niveśita - nijāśritāyai namaḥ

Salutations to Her who raises Her devotees to royal status.

689. ओं राज्यलक्ष्म्यै नमः

Om rājya - lakṣmyai namaḥ

Salutations to Her who is the goddess of sovereignty.

690. ओं कोशनाथायै नमः

Om kośa - nāthāyai namaḥ

Salutations to Her who presides over

treasure or the five sheaths (Kośas) of the human personality.

691. ओं चतुरंग - बलेश्वर्यै नमः

Om catur - aṅga - bal'eśvaryai namaḥ

Salutations to Her who commands armies well - equipped in all the four arms.

692. ओं साम्राज्य - दायिन्यै नमः

Om sāmrājya - dāyinyai namaḥ

Salutations to Her who bestows imperial dominion.

693. ओं सत्यसन्धायै नमः

Om satya - sandhāyai namaḥ

Salutations to Her who is wedded to Truth.

694. ओं सागरमेखलायै नमः

Om sāgara - mekhalāyai namaḥ

Salutations to Her whose girdle is the sea.

695. ओं दीक्षितायै नमः

Om dīkṣitāyai namaḥ

Salutations to Her who is under a holy vow.

696. ओं दैत्यशमन्यै नमः

Om daitya - śamanyai namaḥ

Salutations to Her who quells evil foces.

697. ओं सर्वलोकवशंकर्यै नमः

Om sarva - loka - vaśaṅkaryai namaḥ

Salutations to Her who keeps all the worlds under Her sway.

698. ओं सर्वार्थदात्र्यै नमः

Om sarvārtha - dātryai namaḥ

Salutations to Her who grants all our wants.

699. ओं सावित्र्यै नमः

Om sāvitryai namaḥ

Salutations to Her who is the Creative Power.

700. ओं सच्चिदानन्द - रूपिण्यै नमः

Om sac - cid - ānanda - rūpiṇyai namaḥ

Salutations to Her whose form is Existence - Knowledge - Bliss absolute.

701. ओं देशाकालापरिच्छिन्नायै नमः

Om deśa - kāl'āparicchinnāyai namaḥ

Salutations to Her who is not limited by space and time.

702. ओं सर्वगायै नमः

Om sarvagāyai namaḥ

Salutations to Her who is present in all as the inner controller.

703. ओं सर्वमोहिन्यै नमः

Om sarva - mohinyai namaḥ

Salutations to Her who casts Her spell on all.

704. ओं सरस्वत्यै नमः

Om sarasvatyai namaḥ

Salutations to Her who is Sarasvatī, the Goddess of discriminative wisdom and spiritual illumination.

705. ओं शास्त्रमय्यै नमः

Om śāstramayyai namaḥ

Salutations to Her who is the science of the spirit.

706. ओं गुहांबायै नमः

Om guhāmbāyai namaḥ

Salutations to Her who is the Mother residing in the cave of intelligence (Also the mother of Guha or Subrahmaṇya).

707. ओं गुह्यरूपिण्यै नमः

Om guhya - rūpiṇyai namaḥ

Salutations to Her whose form is subtle.

708. ओं सर्वोपाधि - विनिर्मुक्तायै नमः

Om sarv'opādhi - vinirmuktāyai namaḥ

Salutations to Her who is free from all limitations.

709. ओं सदाशिव - पतिव्रतायै नमः

Om saaāśiva - pativratāyai namaḥ

Salutations to Her who is the devoted Consort of Sadāśiva.

710. ओं संप्रदायेश्वर्यै नमः

Om sampradāy'eśvaryai namaḥ

Salutations to Her who is the guardian of sacred traditions.

711. ओं साधुने नमः

Om sādhune namaḥ

Salutations to Her who is rightly understood as the Power that dispels ignorance.

712. ओं यै नमः

Om yai namaḥ

Salutations to Her who is denoted by the syllable 'ī'.

713. ओं गुरुमण्डल - रूपिण्यै नमः

Om guru - maṇḍala - rūpiṇyai namaḥ

Salutations to Her who embodies in Herself the teaching of successive lines of teachers.

714. ओं कुलोत्तीर्णायै नमः

Om kulottīrṇāyai namaḥ

Salutations to Her who transcends the sphere of the senses, including the mind.

715. ओं भगाराध्यायै नमः

Om bhag'ārādhyāyai namaḥ

Salutations to Her who is worshipped in the orbit of the sun.

716. ओं मायायै नमः

Om māyāyai namaḥ

Salutations to Her who is the Power called Māyā.

717. ओं मधुमत्यै नमः

Om madhumatyai namaḥ

Salutations to Her who is called

Madhumatī, the ultimate step to be taken by the highest Yogins.

718. ओं मह्यै नमः

Om mahyai namaḥ

Salutations to Her who is Mahī, the common ground of all.

719. ओं गणांबायै नमः

Om gaṇāmbāyai namaḥ

Salutations to Her who is the Mother of all the hosts of Śiva and Ganeśa.

720. ओं गुह्यकाराध्यायै नमः

Om guhyak'ārādhyāyai namaḥ

Salutations to Her who is worshipped by the demi - gods called the Guhyakas.

721. ओं कोमलांग्यै नमः

Om komalāṅgyai namaḥ

Salutations to Her whose form is delicate and pleasing.

722. ओं गुरुप्रियायै नमः

Om guru - priyāyai namaḥ

Salutations to Her who is the Consort of Śiva, the great Guru.

723. ओं स्वतन्त्रायै नमः

Om svatantrāyai namaḥ

Salutations to Her who is the only Independent Being.

724. ओं सर्वतन्त्रेश्यै नमः

Om sarva - tantr'eśyai namaḥ

Salutations to Her who is the presiding deity of all the Tantras.

725. ओं दक्षिणामूर्ति - रूपिण्यै नमः

Om dakṣiṇā - mūrti - rūpiṇyai namaḥ

Salutations to Her who has taken the form of Dakṣiṇāmūrti.

726. ओं सनकादि - समाराध्यायै नमः

Om sanakādi - sam'ārādhyāyai namaḥ

Salutations to Her who is worthy of being worshipped by Sanaka and other great ascetics.

727. ओं शिवज्ञान - प्रदायिन्यै नमः

Om śiva - jñāna - pradāyinyai namaḥ

Salutations to Her who imparts the knowledge of the Supreme Being (Śiva).

728. ओं चित्कलायै नमः

Om cit - kalāyai namaḥ

Salutations to Her who is a spark of Divine Consciouness (Citkalā).

729. ओं आनन्द - कलिकायै नमः

Om ānanda - kalikāyai namaḥ

Salutations to Her who is the bud of Divine Bliss.

730. ओं प्रेमरूपायै नमः

Om prema - rūpāyai namaḥ

Salutations to Her who is pure Love itself.

731. ओं प्रियंकर्यै नमः

Om priyaṅkaryai namaḥ

Salutations to Her who grants what is dear to us.

732. ओं नामपारायण - प्रीतायै नमः

Om nāma - pārāyaṇa - prītāyai namaḥ

Salutations to Her who is pleased with a litany of Her names.

733. ओं नन्दिविद्यायै नमः

Om nandi - vidyāyai namaḥ

Salutations to Her who is the Deity of the Mantra of Nandikeśvara.

734. ओं नटेश्वर्यै नमः

Om nateśvaryai namaḥ

Salutations to Her who is the counterpart of Cidambara Naṭeśvara.

735. ओं मिथ्या - जगदधिष्ठानायै नमः

Om mithyā - jagad - adhisthānāyai namaḥ

Salutations to Her who is the ground of the Changing universe.

736. ओं मुक्तिदायै नमः

Om mukti - dāyai namaḥ

Salutations to Her who is the giver of salvation.

737. ओं मुक्तिरूपिण्यै नमः

Om mukti - rūpiṇyai namaḥ

Salutations to Her who is Herself salvation.

738. ओं लास्यप्रियायै नमः

Om lāsya - priyāyai namaḥ

Salutations to Her who likes the rhythmic dance of women, called Lāsya.

739. ओं लयकर्यै नमः

Om laya - karyai namaḥ

Salutations to Her who generates harmony in dance and music.

740. ओं लज्जायै नमः

Om lajjāyai namaḥ

Salutations to Her who is modesty itself.

741. ओं रंभादिवन्दितायै नमः

Om rambh'ādi - vanditāyai namaḥ

Salutations to Her who is adored by Rambhā and other celestial damsels.

742. ओं भवदाव - सुधावृष्ट्यै नमः

Om bhava - dāva - sudhā - vṛṣṭyai namaḥ

Salutations to Her who is the rain of nectar that puts out the wild fire of Samsāra.

743. ओं पापारण्य - दवानलायै नमः

Om pāp'āraṇya - davānalāyai namaḥ

Salutations to Her who is also the wild fire that burns down the jungles of sins.

744. ओं दौर्भाग्य - तूलवातूलायै नमः

Om daurbhāgya - tūla - vātūlāyai namaḥ

Salutations to Her who is the wind that drives away the flakes of misfortune.

745. ओं जराध्वान्तरविप्रभायै नमः

Om jarā - dhvānta - ravi - prabhāyai namaḥ

Salutations to Her who removes by her effulgence the gloom of infirmities attendant on old age.

746. ओं भाग्याब्धि - चन्द्रिकायै नमः

Om bhāgy'ābdhi - candrikāyai namaḥ

Salutations to Her who is the full moon that sets up the tides of good fortune.

747. ओं भक्त-चित्त-केकि-घनाघनायै नमः

Om bhakta - citta - keki - ghanā'ghanāyai namaḥ

Salutations to Her who is heavily water - laden cloud that makes the hearts of devotees dance like peacocks.

748. ओं रोगपर्वत - दंभोलये नमः

Om roga - parvata - dambholaye namaḥ

Salutations to Her who is the thunderbolt that shatters the mountain of diseases.

749. ओं मृत्युदारु - कुठारिकायै नमः

Om mṛtyu - dāru - kuṭhārikāyai namaḥ

Salutations to Her who is the axe that cuts down the tree of death.

750. ओं महेश्वर्यै नमः

Om maheśvaryai namaḥ

Salutations to Her who is the Supreme Sovereign.

751. ओं महाकाल्यै नमः

Om mahā - kālyai namaḥ

Salutations to Her who is Mahākālī — the Divine Mother who consumes everything as Time.

752. ओं महाग्रासायै नमः

Om mahā - grāsāyai namaḥ

Salutations to Her who is the great Devourer.

753. ओं महाशनायै नमः

Om mah'āsanāyai namaḥ

Salutations to Her whose repast consists of this mighty universe.

754. ओं अपर्णायै नमः

Om aparnāyai namaḥ

Salutations to Her who is Aparnā—the one who did not take even a leaf while performing austerities.

755. ओं चण्डिकायै नमः

Om candikāyai namah

Salutations to Her who is the Candikā, the awe - inspiring one.

756. ओं चण्डमुण्डासुर - निषूदिन्यै नमः

Om canda - mund'āsura - nisūdinyai namah

Salutations to Her who is the destroyer of the demons Canda and Munda, and came to be known as Cāmuṇḍā for this reason.

757. ओं क्षराक्षरात्मिकायै नमः

Om kṣar'ākṣar'ātmikāyai namaḥ

Salutations to Her who is both the changeful and the changeless.

758. ओं सर्वलोकेश्यै नमः

Om sarva - lokeśyai namaḥ

Salutations to Her who is the Ruler of all the worlds.

759. ओं विश्वधारिण्यै नमः

Om viśva - dhāriṇyai namaḥ

Salutations to Her who supports the whole universe.

760. ओं त्रिवर्गदात्र्यै नमः

Om tri - varga - dātryai namaḥ

Salutations to Her who bestows the triad of human values (aspiration to do meritorious acts, the capacity for it, and the means for it).

761. ओं सुभगायै नमः

Om subhagāyai namaḥ

Salutations to Her who is the goddess of affluence.

762. ओं त्र्यंबकायै नमः

Om tryambakāyai namaḥ

Salutations to Her who is the three - eyed Goddess.

763. ओं त्रिगुणात्मिकायै नमः

Om triguṇ'ātmikāyai namaḥ

Salutations to Her in whom the three dispositions of Nature are in harmony.

764. ओं स्वर्गापवर्गदायै नमः

Om svarg'āpavargadāyai namaḥ

Salutations to Her who bestows the enjoyments of Paradise and the eternal bliss of Mokṣa.

765. ओं शुद्धायै नमः

Om suddhāyai namaḥ

Salutations to Her who is ever pure.

766. ओं जपापुष्प - निभाकृतये नमः

Om japā - puṣpa - nibh'ākṛtaye namaḥ

Salutations to Her whose colour is of the nature of *japa* flowers (China rose).

767. ओं ओजोवत्यै नमः

Om ojovatyai namaḥ

Salutations to Her who is full of energy.

768. ओं द्युतिधरायै नमः

Om dyuti - dharāyai namaḥ

Salutations to Her who is full of splendour.

769. ओं यज्ञरूपायै नमः

Om yajña - rūpāyai namaḥ

Salutations to Her who is Viṣṇu, the embodiment of sacrifice.

770. ओं प्रियव्रतायै नमः

Om priya - vratāyai namaḥ

Salutations to Her who is fond of holy vows.

771. ओं दुराराध्यायै नमः

Om dur'ārādhyāyai namaḥ

Salutations to Her who is hard to worship by those having no control over the senses.

772. ओं दुराधर्षायै नमः

Om dur'ādharṣāyai namaḥ

Salutations to Her who is hard to resist.

773. ओं पाटली - कुसुम - प्रियायै नमः

Om pāṭalī - kusuma - priyāyai namaḥ

Salutations to Her who is fond of Pāṭalī flower (the pale - red trumpet flowers).

774. ओं महत्यै नमः

Om mahatyai namaḥ

Salutations to Her who is greater than all.

775. ओं मेरुनिलयायै नमः

Om meru - nilayāyai namaḥ

Salutations to Her who resides on Meru.

776. ओं मन्दार - कुसुम - प्रियायै नमः

Om mandāra - kusuma - priyāyai namaḥ

Salutations to Her who loves the Mandāra flowers (coral - tree flowers of heaven).

777. ओं वीराराध्यायै नमः

Om vīr'ārādhyāyai namaḥ

Salutations to Her who is worshipped by the Vīras (the heroic).

778. ओं विराड्रूपायै नमः

Om virāḍ - rūpāyai namah

Salutations to Her who is the Virāt, the Cosmic Whole.

779. ओं विरजसे नमः

Om virajase namaḥ

Salutations to Her who is without any stain.

780. ओं विश्वतोमुख्यै नमः

Om viśvato - mukhyai namaḥ

Salutations to Her who faces all directions.

781. ओं प्रत्यग् - रूपायै नमः

Om pratyag - rūpāyai namaḥ

Salutations to Her who is the Self within

782. ओं पराकाशायै नमः

Om par'ākāśāyai namaḥ

Salutations to Her who is the Transcendental Ether.

783. ओं प्राणदायै नमः

Om prāṇadāyai namaḥ

Salutations to Her who gives life.

784. ओं प्राणरूपिण्यै नमः

Om prāṇa - rūpiṇyai namaḥ

Salutations to Her who is Herself Life (Prāṇa or Brahmā).

785. ओं मार्तण्ड - भैरवाराध्यायै नमः

Om mārtaṇḍa - bhairavā'rādhyāyai namaḥ

Salutations to Her who is adored by Mārtaṇḍa bhairava (a form of Śiva).

786. ओं मन्त्रिणी - न्यस्त - राज्यधुरे नमः

Om mantriṇī - nyasta - rājya - dhure namaḥ

Salutations to Her who has invested her minister (Śyāmalāmbā) with all Her regal authority.

787. ओं त्रिपुरेश्यै नमः

Om tripur'eśyai namaḥ

Salutations to Her who is the deity Tripurā.

788. ओं जयत्सेनायै नमः

Om jayat - senāyai namaḥ

Salutations to Her who has victorious armies at Her command.

789. ओं निस्त्रैगुण्यायै नमः

Om nistraiguṇyāyai namah

Salutations to Her who is devoid of the three dispositions of Nature.

790. ओं परापरायै नमः

Om par'āparāyai namaḥ

Salutations to Her who is both the Absolute and the Relative.

791. ओं सत्यज्ञानानन्द - रूपायै नमः

Om satya - jñān'ānanda - rūpāyai namaḥ

Salutations to Her who is Truth, Knowledge and Bliss.

792. ओं सामरस्य - परायणायै नमः

Om sāmarasya - parāyanāyai namah

Salutations to Her who is the harmony of all Diversities.

793. ओं कपर्दिन्यै नमः

Om kapardinyai namaḥ

Salutations to Her who is the Consort of Kapardin (Śiva).

794. ओं कलामालायै नमः

Om kalā - mālāyai namaḥ

Salutations to Her who wears all arts and crafts as a garland.

795. ओं कामदुहे नमः

Om kāma - duhe namaḥ

Salutations to Her who is a Kāmadug (the wish - yielding celestial Cow) to Her devotees.

796. ओं काम - रूपिण्यै नमः

Om kāma - rūpiṇyai namaḥ

Salutations to Her who can assume any form.

797. ओं कलानिधये नमः

Om kalā - nidhaye namaḥ

Salutations to Her who is the treasury of all arts.

798. ओं काव्यकलायै नमः

Om kāvya - kalāyaï namaḥ

Salutations to Her who is the art of poetry.

799. ओं रसज्ञायै नमः

Om rasa - jñāyai namah

Salutations to Her who knows all Rasas (tastes, values, joys etc.)

800. ओं रसशेवधये नमः

Om rasa - śevadhaye namah

Salutations to Her who is Herself the treasure of all Rasas.

801. ओं पुष्टायै नमः

Om puṣṭāyai namaḥ

Salutations to Her who is full of vigour.

802. ओं पुरातनायै नमः

Om purātanāyai namaḥ

Salutations to Her who is the most Ancient Being.

803. ओं पूज्यायै नमः

Om pujyāyai namah

Salutations to Her who is worthy of devoted worship.

804. ओं पुष्करायै नमः

Om puṣkarāyai namaḥ

Salutations to Her who is like a lotus in bloom.

805. ओं पुष्करेक्षणायै नमः

Om puṣkarekṣaṇāyai namaḥ

Salutations to Her who has eyes charming like petals of lotus.

806. ओं परस्मै ज्योतिषे नमः

Om parasmai jyotiṣe namaḥ

Salutations to Her who is the Supreme Light that illumines all luminaries.

807. ओं परस्मै धाम्ने नमः

Om parasmai dhāmne namaḥ

Salutations to Her who is the Supreme Abode that homes all things that exist.

808. ओं परमाणवे नमः

Om param'āṇave namaḥ

Salutations to Her who is also the subtlest particle.

809. ओं परात्परायै नमः

Om parāt - parāyai namaḥ

Salutations to Her who is the Supermost superior even to Brahmā, Visnu, and Śiva who are adored as supreme deities.

810. ओं पाशहस्तायै नमः

Om pāśahastāyai namah

Salutations to Her who holds in Her hands the noose that binds all to Samsāra.

811. ओं पाशहन्त्र्यै नमः

Om pāśa - hantryai namah

Salutations to Her who cuts the bond of Samsāra.

812. ओं परमन्त्र - विभेदिन्यै नमः

Om para - mantra - vibhedinyai namah

Salutations to Her who breaks the spells of one's enemies.

813. ओं मूर्तायै नमः

Om mūrtāyai namaḥ

Salutations to Her who has forms.

814. ओं अमूर्तायै नमः

Om amūrtāyai namaḥ

Salutations to Her who is formless also.

815. ओं अनित्यतृप्तायै नमः

Om anitya - tṛptāyai namaḥ

Salutations to Her who is satisfied even with our perishable offerings.

816. ओं मुनिमानस - हंसिकायै नमः

Om muni - mānasa - hamsikāyai namaḥ

Salutations to Her the swan who swims in the Mānasa lake of the minds of saints.

817. ओं सत्यव्रतायै नमः

Om satya - vratāyai namaḥ

Salutations to Her who is vowed to truth.

818. ओं सत्यरूपायै नमः

Om satya - rūpāyai namaḥ

Salutations to Her who is herself truth.

819. ओं सर्वान्तर्यामिण्यै नमः

Om sarv'āntar - yāmiṇyai namaḥ

Salutations to Her who is the Inner Ruler of all beings.

820. ओं सत्यै नमः

Om satyai namaḥ

Salutations to Her who is the Eternal Being as also the Consort of Parama - śiva.

821. ओं ब्रह्माण्यै नमः

Om Brahmāṇyai namaḥ

Salutations to Her who is the Śakti of Brahmā the Creator.

822. ओं ब्रह्मणे नमः

Om brahmaṇe namaḥ

Salutations to Her who is Herself Brahmā.

823. ओं जनन्यै नमः

Om jananyai namaḥ

Salutations to Her who is the Mother of the Universe.

824. ओं बहुरूपायै नमः

Om bahu-rūpāyai namaḥ

Salutations to Her who has taken the form of the many.

825. ओं बुधार्चितायै नमः

Om budh'ārcitāyai namaḥ

Salutations to Her who is worshipped by the wise.

826. ओं प्रसवित्र्यै नमः

Om prasavitryai namaḥ

Salutations to Her who gives birth to the universe.

827. ओं प्रचण्डायै नमः

Om pracaṇḍāyai namaḥ

Salutations to Her who is awe-inspiring.

828. ओं आज्ञायै नमः

Om ājñāyai namaḥ

Salutations to Her who is divine commandments.

829. ओं प्रतिष्ठायै नमः

Om pratiṣṭhāyai namaḥ

Salutations to Her who is the foundation of all things.

830. ओं प्रकटाकृतये नमः

Om prakaṭ'ākṛtaye namaḥ

Salutations to Her who is manifest in all as the I-sense.

831. ओं प्राणेश्वर्यै नमः

Om prāṇ'eśvaryai namaḥ

Salutations to Her who is the ruler of Prāṇa (life force).

832. ओं प्राणदात्र्यै नमः

Om prāṇa-dātryai namaḥ

Salutations to Her who gives life.

833. ओं पंचाशत्पीठ-रूपिण्यै नमः

Om pañcāśat-pīṭha-rūpiṇyai namaḥ

Salutations to Her who forms the fifty basic sounds of our speech, or who has fifty centres of worship.

834. ओं विशृंखलायै नमः

Om viśṛṅkhalāyai namaḥ

Salutations to Her who is ever unfettered.

835. ओं विविक्तस्थायै नमः

Om viviktasthāyai namaḥ

Salutations to Her who dwells in the hearts of the wise or in sacred secluded spots.

836. ओं वीरमात्रे नमः

Om vīra-mātre namaḥ

Salutations to Her who is the Mother worshipped by the heroes (Vīras).

837. ओं वियत्प्रसुवे नमः

Om viyat-prasuve namaḥ

Salutations to Her who is the source of Viyat, the substance from which evolution takes place.

838. ओं मुकुन्दायै नमः

Om mukundāyai namaḥ

Salutations to Her who gives salvation to Jīvas.

839. ओं मुक्तिनिलयायै नमः

Om mukti-nilayāyai namaḥ

Salutations to Her who is the Abode of those who attain salvation.

840. ओं मूलविग्रह-रूपिण्यै नमः

Om mūla-vigraha-rūpiṇyai namaḥ

Salutations to Her who is the Root from which all other Śaktis like Bālā have their origin.

841. ओं भावज्ञायै नमः

Om bhāva-jñāyai namaḥ

Salutations to Her who knows all thoughts and sentiments.

842. ओं भवरोगघ्न्यै नमः

Om bhava-rogaghnyai namaḥ

Salutations to Her who can cure the disease of recurring transmigratory existence.

843. ओं भवचक्र-प्रवर्तिन्यै नमः

Om bhava-cakra-pravartinyai namaḥ

Salutations to Her who has also set in motion the wheel of recurring transmigratory existence.

844. ओं छन्दः सारायै नमः

Om chandaḥ-sārāyai namaḥ

Salutations to Her who is the essence of all Vedas.

845. ओं शास्त्रसारायै नमः

Om śāstra-sārāyai namaḥ

Salutations to Her who is the essence of all Śāstras (Scriptures).

846. ओं मन्त्रसारायै नमः

Om mantra-sārāyai namaḥ

Salutations to Her who is the source of all Mantras.

847. ओं तलोदर्यै नमः

Om tal'odaryai namaḥ

Salutations to Her who, though slender of waist, contains within Herself all the Talas, (worlds) like Atala, Vitala and others.

848. ओं उदारकीर्तये नमः

Om udāra-kīrtaye namaḥ

Salutations to Her whose fame extends everywhere.

849. ओं उद्दामवैभवायै नमः

Om uddāma-vaibhavāyai namaḥ

Salutations to Her who is boundless in Her might and glory.

850. ओं वर्णरूपिण्यै नमः

Om varṇa-rūpiṇyai namaḥ

Salutations to Her whose form is denoted by the letters of our language.

851. ओं जन्ममृत्यु-जरातप्त-जन-विश्रान्ति-दायिन्यै नमः

Om janma-mṛtyu-jarā-tapta-jana- viśrānti-dāyinyai namaḥ

Salutations to Her who gives peace and repose to those afflicted with birth, old age and death.

852. ओं सर्वोपनिष-दुद्घुष्टायै नमः

Om sarv'opaniṣad-udghuṣṭāyai namaḥ

Salutations to Her whom all the Upanishads proclaim.

853. ओं शान्त्यतीत-कलात्मिकायै नमः

Om śāntyatīta-kal'ātmikāyai namaḥ

Salutations to Her who transcends even the state of peace.

854. ओं गंभीरायै नमः

Om gambhīrāyai namaḥ

Salutations to Her who is inscrutable.

855. ओं गगनान्तस्थायै नमः

Om gagan'āntasthāyai namaḥ

Salutations to Her who pervades all space.

856. ओं गर्वितायै नमः

Om garvitāyai namaḥ

Salutations to Her who is the Pride of Śiva ('I' as Prakāsa) which is the source of the Creative process.

857. ओं गानलोलुपायै नमः

Om gāna-lolupāyai namaḥ

Salutations to Her who is fond of music.

858. ओं कल्पना-रहितायै नमः

Om kalpanā-rahitāyai namaḥ

Salutations to Her who is untouched by the creative process which proceeds from Her will.

859. ओं काष्ठायै नमः

Om kāṣṭhāyai namaḥ

Salutations to Her who is the Supreme Goal.

860. ओं अकान्तायै नमः

Om akāntāyai namaḥ

Salutations to Her who effaces all sin.

861. ओं कान्तार्ध-विग्रहायै नमः

Om kānt'ārdha-vigrahāyai namaḥ

Salutations to Her who is half the person of Her Consort, Parama-śiva.

862. ओं कार्यकारण-निर्मुक्तायै नमः

Om kārya-kāraṇa-nirmuktāyai namaḥ

Salutations to Her who is not subject to the laws of cause and effect.

863. ओं कामकेलि-तरंगितायै नमः

Om kāma-keli-tarangitāyai namaḥ

Salutations to Her who overflows with joy in the company of Her Lord, Kāmeśvara.

864. ओं कनत्कनक-ताटंकायै नमः

Om kanat-kanaka-tāṭaṅkāyai namaḥ

Salutations to Her who wears ear-ornaments of burnished gold.

865. ओं लीला-विग्रह-धारिण्यै नमः

Om līlā-vigraha-dhāriṇyai namaḥ

Salutations to Her who takes various forms for Her cosmic play.

866. ओं अजायै नमः

Om ajāyai namaḥ

Salutations to Her for whom there is no birth.

867. ओं क्षयविनिर्मुक्तायै नमः

Om kṣaya-vinirmuktāyai namaḥ

Salutations to Her for whom there is no decay also.

868. ओं मुग्धायै नमः

Om mugdhāyai namaḥ

Salutations to Her who is attractive by her artless beauty and innocence.

869. ओं क्षिप्र-प्रसादिन्यै नमः

Om kṣipra-prasādinyai namaḥ

Salutations to Her who is easily pleased.

870. ओं अन्तर्मुख-समाराध्यायै नमः

Om antar-mukha-sam'ārādhyāyai namaḥ

Salutations to Her whose worship is easy for those whose mental gaze is turned inward.

871. ओं बहिर्मुख-सुदुर्लभायै नमः

Om bahir-mukha-sudurlabhāyai namaḥ

Salutations to Her whose worship is difficult for those whose mental gaze goes outwards.

872. ओं त्रय्यै नमः

Om trayyai namaḥ

Salutations to Her who is the three-fold Veda.

873. ओं त्रिवर्ग-निलयायै नमः

Om trivarga-nilayāyai namaḥ

Salutations to Her who is implicit in the threefold aim of life (Dharma, Artha, and Kāma).

874. ओं त्रिस्थायै नमः

Om tristhāyai namaḥ

Salutations to Her who is present in the three periods of existence like past, present and future.

875. ओं त्रिपुर-मालिन्यै नमः

Om tripura-mālinyai namaḥ

Salutations to Her who is the Deity of the threefold circles in the Śrī-Cakra.

876. ओं निरामयायै नमः

Om nir'āmayāyai namaḥ

Salutations to Her who is free from the ills of life.

877. ओं निरालम्बायै नमः

Om nir'ālambāyai namaḥ

Salutations to Her who depends on none.

878. ओं स्वात्मारामायै नमः

Om sv'ātm'ārāmāyai namaḥ

Salutations to Her who is merged in the joy of Her own Self.

879. ओं सुधासृत्यै नमः

Om sudhāsṛtyai namah

Salutations to Her who is the source of Sudhā (spiritual nectar).

880. ओं संसारपंक-निर्मग्न-समुद्धरण-पण्डितायै नमः

Om samsāra-paṅka-nirmagna-samuddharaṇa-paṇḍitāyai namaḥ

Salutations to Her who is skilled in rescuing men who are sunk in the mire of Samsāra.

881. ओं यज्ञप्रियायै नमः

Om yajña-priyāyai namah

Salutations to Her who delights in acts of sacrifice.

882. ओं यज्ञकर्त्र्यै नमः

Om yajña-kartryai namaḥ

Salutations to Her who directs all sacrificial acts.

883. ओं यजमान-स्वरूपिण्यै नमः

Om yajamāna-svarūpiṇyai namaḥ

Salutations to Her who takes the form of the institutor of sacrifice.

884. ओं धर्माधारायै नमः

Om dharm'ādhārāyai namaḥ

Salutations to Her who is the support of Dharma.

885. ओं धनाध्यक्षायै नमः

Om dhan'ādhyakṣāyai namaḥ

Salutations to Her who controls all riches.

886. ओं धनधान्य-विवर्धिन्यै नमः

Om dhana-dhānya-vivardhinyai namaḥ

Salutations to Her who increases riches and harvests.

887. ओं विप्रप्रियायै नमः

Om vipra-priyāyai namaḥ

Salutations to Her who loves the learned.

888. ओं विप्ररूपायै नमः

Om vipra-rūpāyai namaḥ

Salutations to Her who is Herself the learned.

889. ओं विश्वभ्रमण-कारिण्यै नमः

Om viśva-bhramaṇa-kāriṇyai namaḥ

Salutations to Her who causes, the universe to revolve in cyclic motion.

890. ओं विश्वग्रासायै नमः

Om viśva-grāsāyai namaḥ

Salutations to Her who devours the universe at the end of the cycle.

891. ओं विद्रुमाभायै नमः

Om vidrum'ābhāyai namaḥ

Salutations to Her who is like coral in complexion.

892. ओं वैष्णव्यै नमः

Om vaiṣṇavyai namaḥ

Salutations to Her who is Vaiṣṇavī, the Power of Viṣṇu.

893. ओं विष्णुरूपिण्यै नमः

Om viṣṇu-rūpiṇyai namaḥ

Salutations to Her who is Herself in the form of Viṣṇu.

894. ओं अयोन्यै नमः

Om ayonyai namaḥ

Salutations to Her who has no source other than Herself.

895. ओं योनि-निलयायै नमः

Om yoni-nilayāyai namaḥ

Salutations to Her who houses the power that generates everything.

896. ओं कूटस्थायै नमः

Om kūṭasthāyai namaḥ

Salutations to Her who is the changeless.

897. ओं कुलरूपिण्यै नमः

Om kula-rūpinyai namaḥ

Salutations to Her who is the Deity of the Kaula sect.

898. ओं वीरगोष्ठी-प्रियायै नमः

Om vīra-goṣṭhī-priyāyai namaḥ

Salutations to Her who is fond of the assembly of the devotees of the heroic mode of worship.

899. ओं वीरायै नमः

Om vīrāyai namaḥ

Salutations to Her who is Herself the Hero.

900. ओं नैष्कर्म्यायै नमः

Om naiṣkarmyāyai namah

Salutations to Her who transcends work (Karma).

901. ओं नादरूपिण्यै नमः

Om nāda-rūpiṇyai namaḥ

Salutations to Her who is the primal mystic sound.

902. ओं विज्ञानकलनायै नमः

Om vijñāna-kalanāyai namaḥ

Salutations to Her who is realisation of the Absolute.

903. ओं कल्यायै नमः

Om kalyāyai namah

Salutations to Her who is one to be reckoned with.

904. ओं विदग्धायै नमः

Om vidagdhāyai namah

Salutations to Her who is the wisdom displayed in all skills.

905. ओं बैन्दवासनायै नमः

Om baindav'āsanāyai namaḥ

Salutations to Her who is seated in the Bindu, the central dot in the Śrī-cakra.

906. ओं तत्त्वाधिकायै नमः

Om tattv'ādhikāyai namaḥ

Salutations to Her who transcends all cosmic categories.

907. ओं तत्त्वमय्यै नमः

Om tattva-mayyai namaḥ

Salutations to Her who comprehends all cosmic categories.

908. ओं तत्त्वमर्थ-स्वरूपिण्यै नमः

Om tat-tvam-artha-svarūpiṇyai namaḥ

Salutations to Her who is one with the non-dual Being denoted by the words Tat and Tvam in the great Vedic sentence Tat tvam asi.

909. ओं सामगान-प्रियायै नमः

Om sāma-gāna-priyāyai namaḥ

Salutations to Her who loves the chanting of Sāmaveda.

910. ओं सोम्यायै नमः

Om somyāyai namaḥ

Salutations to Her who is the object of worship in Soma sacrifice.

911. ओं सदाशिव-कुटुंबिन्यै नमः

Om sadāśiva-kuṭumbinyai namaḥ

Salutations to Her who is the Consort of Sadāśiva.

912. ओं सव्यापसव्य-मार्गस्थायै नमः

Om savy'āpasavya-mārgasthāyai namaḥ

Salutations to Her who is reached by both the paths—Savya (samaya) and Apasavya (kaula).

913. ओं सर्वापद्विनिवारिण्यै नमः

Om sarvāpad-vinivāriṇyai namaḥ

Salutations to Her who wards off all dangers.

914. ओं स्वस्थायै नमः

Om svasthāyai namaḥ

Salutation to Her who is established in Herself.

915. ओं स्वभावमधुरायै नमः

Om svabhāva-madhurāyai namah

Salutations to Her who is sweet by nature.

916. ओं धीरायै नमः

Om dhīrāyai namaḥ

Salutations to Her who is endowed with wisdom.

917. ओं धीरसमर्च्चितायै नमः

Om dhīra-samarcitāyai namaḥ

Salutations to Her who is worshipped by the wise with care and completeness.

918. ओं चैतन्यार्घ्य-समाराध्यायै नमः

Om caitany'ārghya-samārādhyāyai namaḥ

Salutations to Her who is best worshipped with the offereings of the spirit as Arghya.

919. ओं चैतन्य-कुसुम-प्रियायै नमः

Om caitanya-kusuma-priyāyai namaḥ

Salutations to Her who loves the flower offerings of the spirit.

920. ओं सदोदितायै नमः

Om sadoditāyai namah

Salutations to Her who is ever shining.

921. ओं सदातुष्टायै नमः

Om sadā-tuṣṭāyai namaḥ

Salutations to Her who is ever pleased.

922. ओं तरुणादित्य-पाटलायै नमः

Om taruṇ'āditya-pāṭalāyai namaḥ

Salutations to Her who is rosy like the morning sun.

923. ओं दक्षिणा-दक्षिणाराध्यायै नमः

Om dakṣiṇ'ādakṣiṇ'ārādhyāyai namaḥ

Salutations to Her who is worshipped according to both the Dakṣiṇācāra and its opposite, by the learned and the unlearned.

924. ओं दरस्मेर-मुखांबुजायै नमः

Om dara-smera-mukh'āmbujāyai namaḥ

Salutations to Her whose smiling face gladdens all.

925. ओं कौलिनी-केवलायै नमः

Om kaulinī-kevalāyai namah

Salutations to Her who is the ultimate object of Kaula worship.

926. ओं अनर्घ्य-कैवल्य-पद-दायिन्यै नमः

Om anarghya-kaivalya-pada-dāyinyai namaḥ

Salutations to Her who confers the priceless state of ultimate bliss and freedom.

927. ओं स्तोत्र-प्रियायै नमः

Om stotra-priyāyai namaḥ

Salutations to Her who loves hymns of praise.

928. ओं स्तुतिमत्यै नमः

Om stuti-matyai namaḥ

Salutations to Her who is worthy of hymns of praise.

929. ओं श्रुति-संस्तुत-वैभवायै नमः

Om śruti-saṃstuta-vaibhavāyai namaḥ

Salutations to Her whose glory is praised by the Vedas.

930. ओं मनस्विन्यै नमः

Om manasvinyai namaḥ

Salutations to Her who is self-possessed.

931. ओं मानवत्यै नमः

Om mānavatyai namaḥ

Salutations to Her who is high-minded.

932. ओं महेश्यै नमः

Om maheśyai namaḥ

Salutations to Her who is the great Queen.

933. ओं मगंलाकृतये नमः

Om maṅgalākṛtaye namaḥ

Salutations to Her with a benign form.

934. ओं विश्वमात्रे नमः

Om viśva-mātre namaḥ

Salutations to Her who is the Mother of the Universe.

935. ओं जगद्धात्र्यै नमः

Om jagad-dhātryai namaḥ

Salutations to Her who is the protectress of the universe.

936. ओं विशालाक्ष्यै नमः

Om viśālākṣyai namaḥ

Salutations to Her who has large eyes or who is worshipped as Viśālākṣī at Kāśī.

937. ओं विरागिण्यै नमः

Om virāgiṇyai namaḥ

Salutations to Her who is utterly passionless.

938. ओं प्रगल्भायै नमः

Om pragalbhāyai namaḥ

Salutations to Her who is surprisingly daring.

939. ओं परमोदारायै नमः

Om param'odārāyai namaḥ

Salutations to Her who is supremely generous.

940. ओं परामोदायै नमः

Om parā-modāyai namaḥ

Salutations to Her who is supremely joyful.

941. ओं मनोमय्यै नमः

Om mano'mayyai namaḥ

Salutations to Her who is all spirit.

942. ओं व्योमकेश्यै नमः

Om vyoma-keśyai namaḥ

Salutations to Her who has the skies above as Her locks of hair on the head.

943. ओं विमानस्थायै नमः

Om vimānasthāyai namaḥ

Salutations to Her who is seated high in Her celestial car.

944. ओं वज्रिण्यै नमः

Om vajriṇyai namaḥ

Salutations to Her who is Indrāṇī.

945. ओं वामकेश्वर्यै नमः

Om vāmakeśvaryai namah

Salutations to Her who is the deity of the leftward path of the Kaulas.

946. ओं पंचयज्ञ-प्रियायै नमः

Om pañca-yajña-priyāyai namaḥ

Salutations to Her who loves the five sacrifices of the rightward Savyā path.

947. ओं पंचप्रेत-मंचाधिशायिन्यै नमः

Om pañca-preta-mañc'ādhi-śāyinyai namaḥ

Salutations to Her who is seated on a seat supported by the Five Dead, (Brahmā, Viṣṇu, Rudra, Īśvara and Sadāśiva).

948. ओं पंचम्यै नमः

Om pañcamyai namaḥ

Salutations to Her who is the Consort of the Fifth of these (Sadāśiva).

949. ओं पंचभूतेश्यै नमः

Om pañca-bhūteśyai namaḥ

Salutations to Her who rules over the five primordial elements.

950. ओं पंचसंख्योपचारिण्यै नमः

Om pañca-saṅkhyo'pacāriṇyai namaḥ

Salutations to Her who is worshipped with the fivefold offering.

951. ओं शाश्वत्यै नमः

Om śāśvatyai namaḥ

Salutations to Her who is eternal.

952. ओं शाश्वतैश्वर्यायै नमः

Om sāśvat'aiśvaryāyai namaḥ

Salutations to Her whose dominion is eternal.

953. ओं शर्मदायै नमः

Om śarmadāyai namaḥ

Salutations to Her who gives eternal happiness.

954. ओं शंभुमोहिन्यै नमः

Om śambhu-mohinyai namaḥ

Salutations to Her who is the charmer of Śambhu, Her Consort.

955. ओं धरायै नमः

Om dharāyai namaḥ

Salutations to Her who is earth on which all beings rest.

956. ओं धरसुतायै नमः

Om dhara-sutāyai namaḥ

Salutations to Her who is the daughter of Himavān, the king of mountains.

957. ओं धन्यायै नमः

Om dhanyāyai namaḥ

Salutations to Her who is supremely blessed.

958. ओं धर्मिण्यै नमः

Om dharmiṇyai namaḥ

Salutations to Her who is righteous.

959. ओं धर्मवर्धिन्यै नमः

Om dharma-vardhinyai namaḥ

Salutations to Her who promotes righteousness in devotees.

960. ओं लोकातीतायै नमः

Om lok'ātītāyai namaḥ

Salutations to Her who transcends all the worlds.

961. ओं गुणातीतायै नमः

Om guṇ'ātītāyai namaḥ

Salutations to Her who transcends the three Guṇas of Prakṛti known as Sattva, Rajas and Tamas.

962. ओं सर्वातीतायै नमः

Om sarv'ātītāyai namaḥ

Salutations to Her who transcends every thing.

963. ओं शमात्मिकायै नमः

Om śam'ātmikāyai namaḥ

Salutations to Her who is the soul of peace.

964. ओं बन्धूक-कुसुम-प्रख्यायै नमः

Om bandhūka-kusuma-prakhyāyai namaḥ

Salutations to Her who has the tender grace of Bandhūka blossoms.

965. ओं बालायै नमः

Om bālāyai namaḥ

Salutations to Her who is eternally young.

966. ओं लीला-विनोदिन्यै नमः

Om līlā-vinodinyai namaḥ

Salutations to Her who sports in the creation of the universe.

967. ओं सुमंगल्यै नमः

Om sumaṅgalyai namaḥ

Salutations to Her who is most auspicious in Herself.

968. ओं सुखकर्यै नमः

Om sukha-karyai namaḥ

Salutations to Her who bestows happiness.

969. ओं सुवेषाढ्यायै नमः

Om suveṣāḍhyāyai namaḥ

Salutations to Her who is gracefully attired.

970. ओं सुवासिन्यै नमः

Om suvāsinyai namaḥ

Salutations to Her who is ever with Her consort.

971. ओं सुवासिन्यर्चन-प्रीतायै नमः

Om suvāsiny'arcana-prītāyai namaḥ

Salutations to Her who is pleased with respect shown to married women.

972. ओं आशोभनायै नमः

Om āśobhanāyai namaḥ

Salutations to Her whose splendour beams forth in all directions.

973. ओं शुद्ध-मानसायै नमः

Om śuddha-mānasāyai namaḥ

Salutations to Her who is ever pure in mind.

974. ओं बिन्दु-तर्पण-सन्तुष्टायै नमः

Om bindu-tarpaṇa-santuṣṭāyai namaḥ

Salutations to Her who is pleased with libations offered to the Bindu (the central dot in the Śrī-cakra).

975. ओं पूर्वजायै नमः

Om pūrva-jāyai namaḥ

Salutations to Her who is the first born.

976. ओं त्रिपुरांबिकायै नमः

Om tripur'āmbikāyai namaḥ

Salutations to Her who is the Mother-Goddess Tripurāmbikā (who represents the stresses in the creative process known Nāda, Bindu, and Kalā).

977. ओं दशमुद्रा-समाराध्यायै नमः

Om daśa- mudrā-sam'ārādhyāyai namaḥ

Salutations to Her who is worshipped through the ten Mudras or signs and poses of the hands and fingers in worship.

978. ओं त्रिपुराश्रीवशंकर्यै नमः

Om tripurāśrī-vaśaṅkaryai namaḥ

Salutations to Her who controls Tripuraśrī (a powerful Deity) presiding over the fifth āvaraṇa called sarvārthasādhaka cakra.

979. ओं ज्ञानमुद्रायै नमः

Om jñāna-mudrāyai namaḥ

Salutations to Her who is jñāna-mudrā also known as Cin-mudrā — the finger-pose of knowledge.

980. ओं ज्ञानगम्यायै नमः

Om jñāna-gamyāyai namaḥ

Salutations to Her who is attained through knowledge.

981. ओं ज्ञान-ज्ञेय-स्वरूपिण्यै नमः

Om jñāna-jñeya-svarūpiṇyai namaḥ

Salutations to Her who is both knowledge and the object of knowledge.

982. योनिमुद्रायै नमः

Om yoni-mudrāyai namaḥ

Salutations to Her who is the finger-pose of creation as well (Yoni-mudrā).

983. ओं त्रिखण्डेश्यै नमः

Om trikhaṇḍ'eśyai namaḥ

Salutations to Her who is the presiding deity of the Trikhaṇḍa, the three regions of Brahmarandhra, Maṇipūra and Mūlādhāra.

984. ओं त्रिगुणायै नमः

Om triguṇāyai namaḥ

Salutations to Her who is endowed with the three modes of Sattva, Rajas and Tamas.

985. ओं अम्बायै नमः

Om ambāyai namaḥ

Salutations to Her who is Ambā, the mother of all.

986. ओं त्रिकोणगायै नमः

Om trikoṇagāyai namaḥ

Salutations to Her who dwells in the triangle of Śrī-cakra.

987. ओं अनघायै नमः

Om anaghāyai namaḥ

Salutations to Her who is sinless.

988. ओं अद्भुत-चारित्रायै नमः

Om adbhuta-cāritrāyai namaḥ

Salutations to Her whose ways are marvellous.

989. ओं वांछितार्थ-प्रदायिन्यै नमः

Om vāñchit'ārtha-pradāyinyai namaḥ

Salutations to Her who grants worshippers whatever they want.

990. ओं अभ्यासातिशय-ज्ञातायै नमः

Om abhyās'ātiśaya-jñātāyai namaḥ

Salutations to Her who is known only through the strenuous practice of spiritual disciplines.

991. ओं षडध्वातीत-रूपिण्यै नमः

Om ṣaḍadhv'ātīta-rūpiṇyai namaḥ

Salutations to Her who transcends the six modes of devotion (Varṇa, Pada, Mantra, Kalā, Tattva, and Buvana).

992. ओं अव्याज-करुणा-मूर्तये नमः

Om avyāja-karuṇā-mūrtaye namaḥ

Salutations to Her who is unconditional grace.

993. ओं अज्ञान-ध्वान्त-दीपिकायै नमः

Om ajñāna-dhvānta-dīpikāyai namaḥ

Salutations to Her who dispels the darkness of ignorance.

994. ओं आबाल-गोप-विदितायै नमः

Om ābāla-gopa-viditāyai namaḥ

Salutations to Her who can be understood by all, even by a child or a cowherd.

995. ओं सर्वानुल्लंघ्य-शासनायै नमः

Om sarv'ānullaṅghya-śāsanāyai namaḥ

Salutations to Her whose laws none dares to transgress.

996. ओं श्रीचक्रराज-निलयायै नमः

Om śrīcakra-rāja-nilayāyai namaḥ

Salutations to Her who dwells in the sovereign Śrī-cakra.

997. ओं श्रीमत्-त्रिपुरसुन्दर्यै नमः

Om śrīmat-tripura-sundaryai namaḥ

Salutations to Her who is the divine Tripura-sundarī.

998. ओं श्रीशिवायै नमः

Om śrī-śivāyai namaḥ

Salutations to Her who is the blessed Śivā (who is identical with Śiva).

999. ओं शिव-शक्त्यैक्य-रूपिण्यै नमः

Om śiva-śakty'aikya-rūpiṇyai namaḥ

Salutations to Her who is the unity of Śiva and Śakti.

1000. ओं ललितांबिकायै नमः

Om lalitāmbikāyai namaḥ

Salutations to Her who is called Lalitāmbika (the goddess who is Lalita, the playful) because Her Cosmic functions are just like a sport to Her, and Ambikā because she is the Mother of all.

(इति श्री ब्रह्माण्डपुराणे उत्तरखण्डे
श्री हयग्रीवागस्त्य-संवादे
श्री ललितासहस्रनाम-स्तोत्र-कथनं संपूर्णम्)

iti śrī brahmāṇḍapurāṇe uttarakhaṇḍe
śrī hayagrīv'āgastya saṃvāde
śrī lalitāsahasranāma stotra kathanam sampūrṇam

Thus ends the narration of Śrī lalitāsahasranāma stotra during the dialogue between Hayagrīva and Agastya, which occurs in the Uttarakhaṇḍa of Śrī Brahmāṇḍapurāṇa.